'EKOLU
3 STRING UKULELE
STRUMMING MASTERY

UKELIKETHEPROS
© 2024 Terry Carter

ISBN-13: **9781958192153**
UKELIKETHEPROS.COM
© 2024 TERRY CARTER

TABLE OF CONTENTS

'EKOLU UKULELE STRUMMING MASTERY	01
TECHNIQUE #1 - A minor	04
TECHNIQUE #2 - C - C - Amin - Amin	05
TECHNIQUE #3 - C - C - Amin - F	06
TECHNIQUE #4 - Amin - Amin - C - G	07
TECHNIQUE #5 - G - D - Amin - C	08
TECHNIQUE #6 - Emin - C - G - D	09
TECHNIQUE #7 - C - F - C - G	10
TECHNIQUE #8 - Shine On	11
TECHNIQUE #9 - C - F - G - Gsus4	12
TECHNIQUE #10 - C - Csus4 - Bb - Bbsus4	13
TECHNIQUE #11 - Bayliner	15
TECHNIQUE #12 - I Won't Hesitate	17
TECHNIQUE #13 - Lemon Drops	19
TECHNIQUE #14 - Yellow Canary's	21
TECHNIQUE #15 - Sancho's Revenge	22
TECHNIQUE #16 - Hawaiian VAMP	23
TECHNIQUE #17 - Hawaiian Noho Pai Pai	25
TECHNIQUE #18 - Diatonic Chords (C)	27
TECHNIQUE #19 - Diatonic Chords (G)	29
WHAT'S NEXT?	31
THE ESSENTIALS	A
HOW TO READ TAB	B
NOTES ON THE 'EKOLU UKULELE NECK	C
'EKOLU HANDS	D
'EKOLU UKULELE PARTS	E
UNDERSTANDING 'EKOLU CHORD DIAGRAMS	F
'EKOLU CHORD CHART	G
MUSIC SYMBOLS TO KNOW - EKOLU	I
ABOUT THE AUTHOR	K
ABOUT UKE LIKE THE PROS	L
ABOUT TERRY CARTER MUSIC STORE	M

'EKOLU
3 STRING UKULELE
STRUMMING MASTERY

Welcome to the 'Ekolu 3 String Ukulele Strumming Mastery book! This is an invitation to explore the boundless possibilities of a truly unique instrument. The 'Ekolu, a 3-string marvel designed by six-time Grammy winner Daniel Ho in collaboration with Pepe Romero Jr. and Romero Creations, is redefining the ukulele experience. With its innovative design, the 'Ekolu simplifies the art of playing while opening up new realms of creativity and musical expression. The 'Ekolu, which means "three" in Hawaiian, offers a refreshing take on the traditional ukulele by omitting the 4th or G string, leaving you with just three strings to work with, C - E - A. But don't let the reduced string count fool you—this instrument retains the full, warm sound of a standard ukulele while making playability easier than ever. Whether you're a complete beginner or a seasoned player, the 'Ekolu is designed to help you focus on what really matters: rhythm, groove, and the pure joy of making music.

Imagine an instrument that strips away complexity, allowing you to dive right into the heart of the music. That's the 'Ekolu. With fewer strings to manage, you can concentrate on developing your strumming techniques, mastering chord transitions, and truly immersing yourself in the music. The simplicity of the 'Ekolu doesn't just make it easier to play—it makes it easier to create. The 'Ekolu Ukulele is a gateway to a new musical experience. Here's why this course and the 'Ekolu itself are perfect for musicians at any level.

The 'Ekolu Ukulele is ideal for those who are just starting their musical journey, as well as for experienced players looking to simplify and refine their technique. The reduced string count eliminates unnecessary complexity, allowing you to focus on perfecting your rhythm and groove. Chord progressions become a breeze on the 'Ekolu. The three-string setup makes it easier to learn and switch between chords, helping you build confidence as you explore new musical styles. Despite its innovative design, the 'Ekolu maintains the rich, resonant sound that you love about the traditional ukulele. You'll enjoy the familiar warmth of the ukulele's tone, with the added benefit of enhanced playability.

The 'Ekolu 3 String Ukulele Strumming Mastery book is thoughtfully designed to guide you through the essentials of playing this unique instrument. The book starts with foundational lessons, introducing you to the basic strumming patterns and chord structures. As you progress, you'll tackle more complex rhythms and intricate chord progressions, all tailored to the three-string setup of the 'Ekolu.

You'll begin by getting to know your instrument, understanding its unique features, and learning why the 'Ekolu is such a game-changer for musicians. The course will then lead you through basic chords and strumming patterns, starting with simple yet effective strumming techniques like the D-D-D and D-DU-D patterns, perfect for beginners looking to build a solid foundation. As you advance, you'll explore more dynamic strumming patterns such as D-D-DUDU and the Island Strum, and learn how to smoothly transition between chords like C, Am, F, and G.

For those ready to challenge themselves, the book offers advanced techniques that include strumming styles like the Shine On Strum (D-DU-D-DU) and the Bayliner Strum (D-DX-UXU), which will further refine your playing skills. You'll also have the opportunity to apply what you've learned to classic tunes and new compositions like "Lemon Drops," "Yellow Canary's," "Sancho's Revenge," and "Hawaiian Noho Pai Pai." These songs will not only enrich your repertoire but also demonstrate the versatility of the 'Ekolu. Moreover, the book will help you unlock the secrets of diatonic chords in the keys of C and G, which are fundamental to many popular songs, empowering you to play a wide range of music with confidence.

The 'Ekolu Ukulele isn't just about simplifying your playing; it's about enhancing your creativity. With fewer strings to manage, you're free to experiment with rhythms, explore new sounds, and develop your unique musical style. The 'Ekolu invites you to think differently about music, offering a fresh perspective that encourages innovation and self-expression. Whether you're jamming with friends, playing solo, or composing your own pieces, the 'Ekolu is a tool that will inspire you to push the boundaries of what's possible. Its ease of play makes it accessible to anyone, while its depth and versatility ensure that even the most experienced musicians will find new challenges and opportunities for growth.

The 'Ekolu Ukulele Strumming Mastery book is more than just a series of lessons—it's an adventure in music-making. By the end of this book, you'll not only be proficient in strumming the 'Ekolu, but you'll also have a deeper understanding of how to create and enjoy music with this extraordinary instrument. Whether you're here to learn the basics or to take your ukulele playing to the next level, this book is designed to meet you where you are and help you achieve your musical goals.

The 'Ekolu offers a new way to experience the joy of music, and we're excited to share this journey with you. So, what are you waiting for? Grab your 'Ekolu, tune those three strings, and let's start strumming our way to mastery together. Take the first step toward discovering the magic of the 'Ekolu Ukulele!

THE 'EKOLU
Pronounced: ā-kŏ'-lŭ

The 'Ekolu is a unique musical instrument designed by six-time Grammy Award winner Daniel Ho. It is a version of the ukulele that features only three strings, inspired by traditional three-stringed instruments from various cultures, such as the Mongolian doshpuluur and the Japanese shamisen. The 'Ekolu simplifies the ukulele by omitting the 4th or G string (leaving the C - E - A strings), making it easier to play, especially for beginners and those looking for a more straightforward approach to creating music. Despite the reduction in strings, the 'Ekolu maintains the same musical range as a standard ukulele and is capable of producing the same rich, full sound.

The creation of the 'Ekolu was a collaborative effort between Daniel Ho and master luthier Pepe Romero Jr. Together, they developed the instrument to not only cater to beginners but also to offer advanced players a new way to explore melodies and harmonies. The 'Ekolu's design allows for smoother chord transitions and greater flexibility in playing, particularly in complex keys that are challenging on a four-string ukulele. This innovative instrument opens up new possibilities in music, providing an accessible–yet sophisticated–tool for both novice and seasoned musicians.

Image: Daniel Ho.

STRUMMING TECHNIQUE #1
A minor

This lesson uses the "Amin" chord which uses all open strings. The strum pattern is quarter note - quarter note - half note, using all Down strokes. The quarter notes get one beat while the half note rings out for two beats.

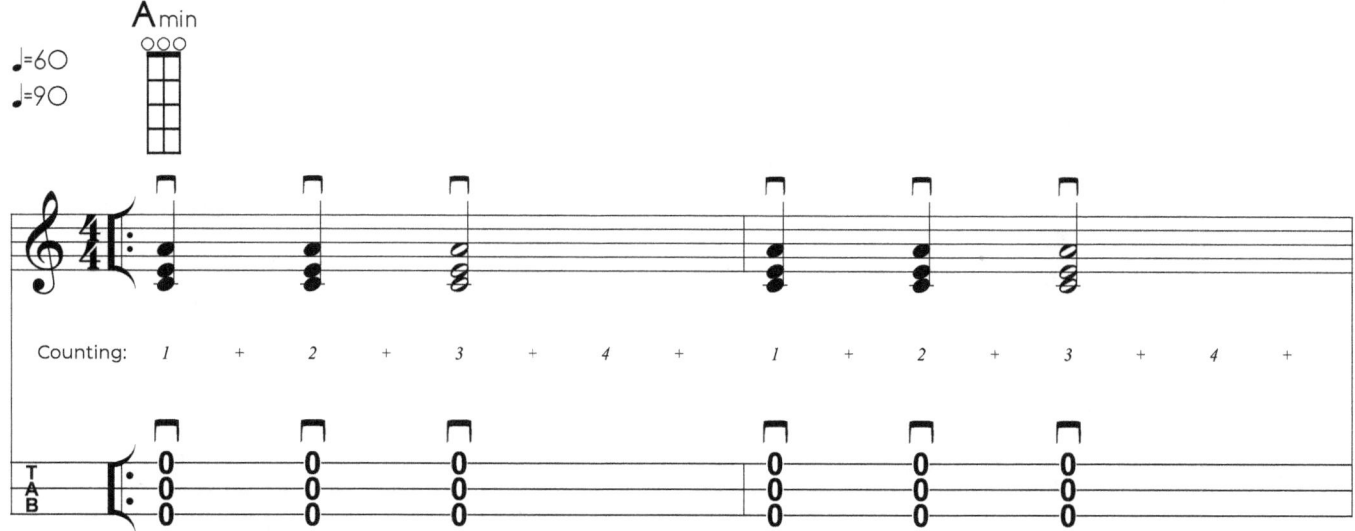

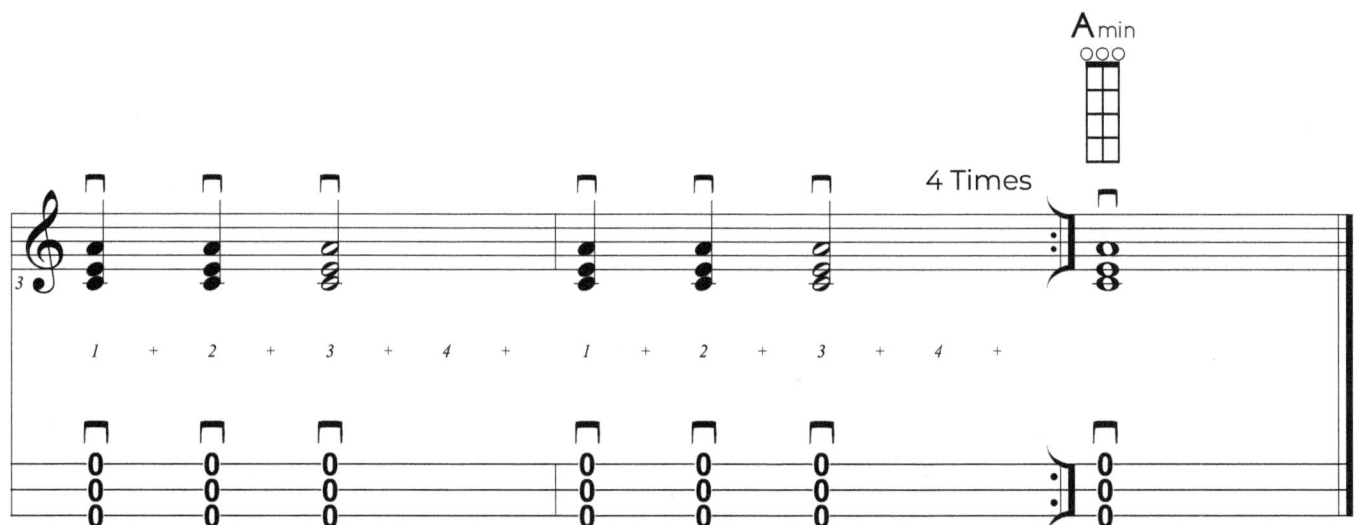

STRUMMING TECHNIQUE #2
C - C - Amin - Amin

This lesson uses the "C" and the "Amin" chords. Each chord will be played for two measures. The strum pattern is quarter note - two eighth notes - half note. The strum direction is Down-Down-Up-Down.

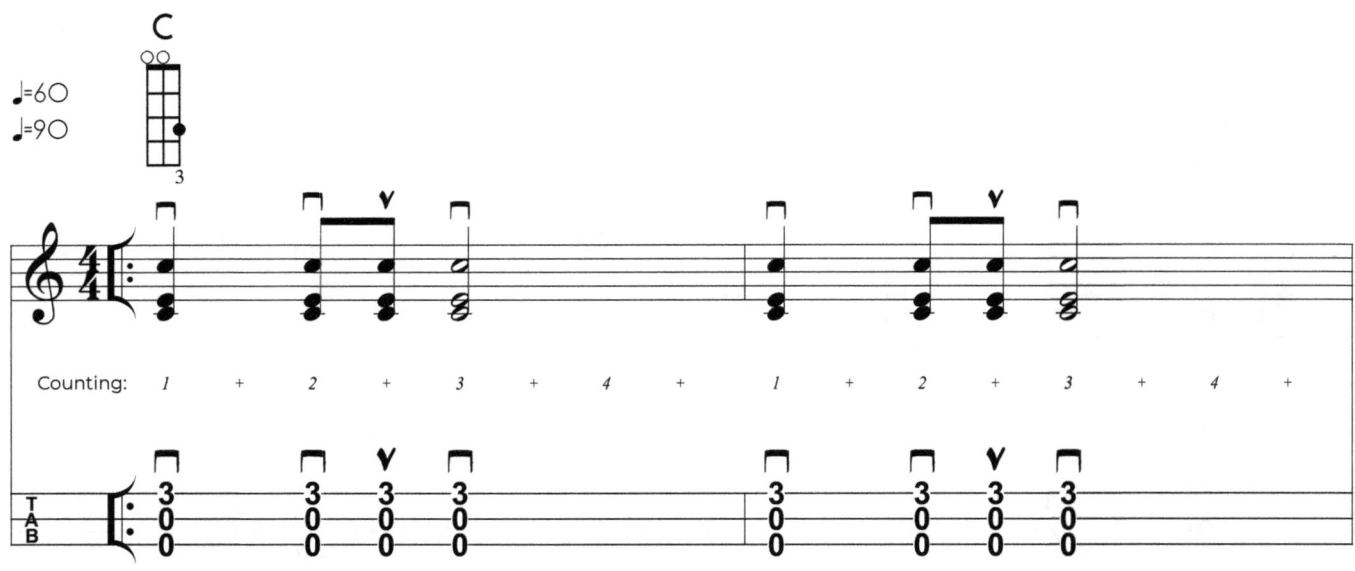

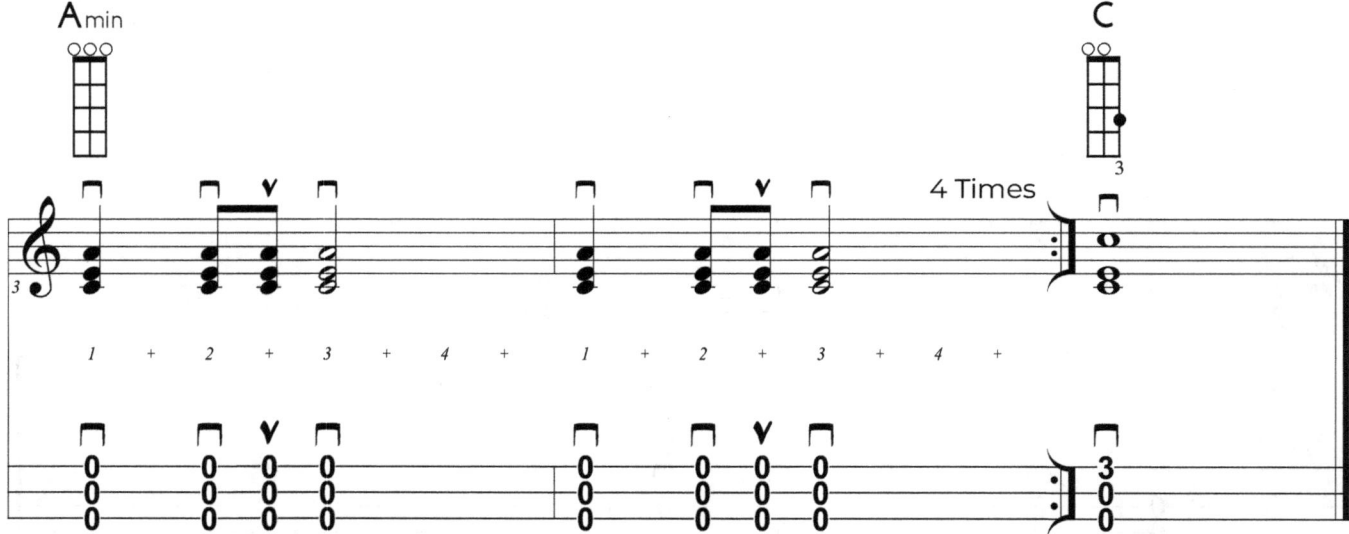

STRUMMING TECHNIQUE #3
C - C - Amin - F

This lesson uses the "C," "Amin," and "F" chords. The "C" chord is played for two measures and the "Amin" and "F" are played for one measure. The strum pattern is quarter note – two eighth notes – quarter note – quarter note. Use a Down-Up strum on the eighth notes.

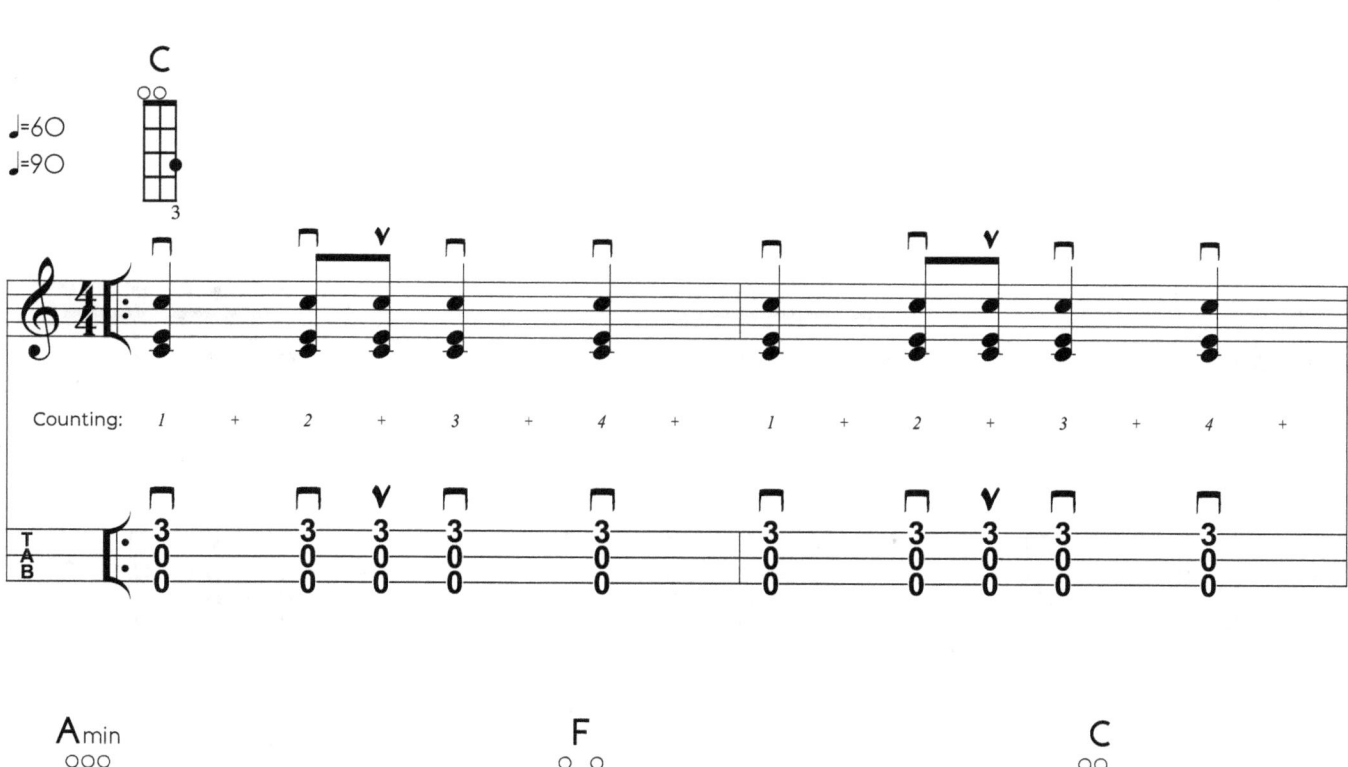

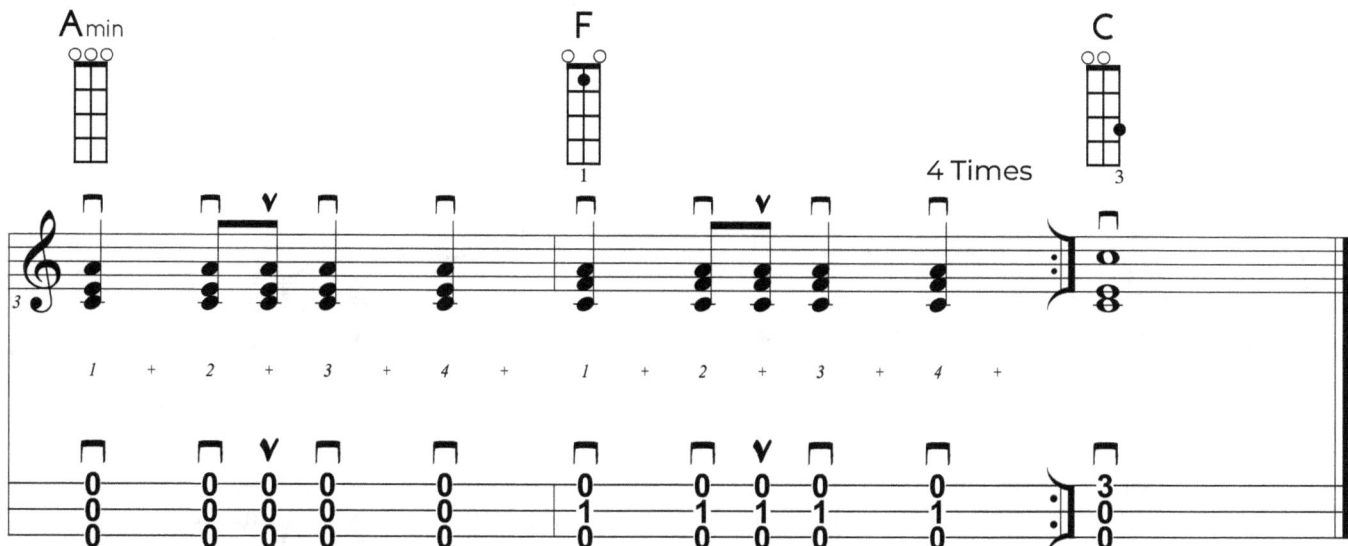

STRUMMING TECHNIQUE #4

Amin - Amin - C - G

This lesson uses the "Amin," "C," and "G" chords. The "Amin" chord is played for two measures and the "C" and "G" are played for one measure. The strum pattern is quarter note – quarter note – four eighth notes. Use Down strums on the quarter notes and Down-Up on the eighth notes.

STRUMMING TECHNIQUE #5
G - D - Amin - C

This lesson uses the "G," "D," "Amin," and "C" chords. Each chord is played for one measure. The strum pattern is quarter note – two eighth notes - quarter note – two eighth notes. Use Down strums on the quarter notes and Down-Up on the eighth notes.

STRUMMING TECHNIQUE #6
Emin - C - G - D

This lesson uses the "Emin," "C," "G," and "D" chords. Each chord is played for one measure. The strum pattern is quarter note – six eighth notes. Use Down strums on the quarter notes and Down-Up on the eighth notes.

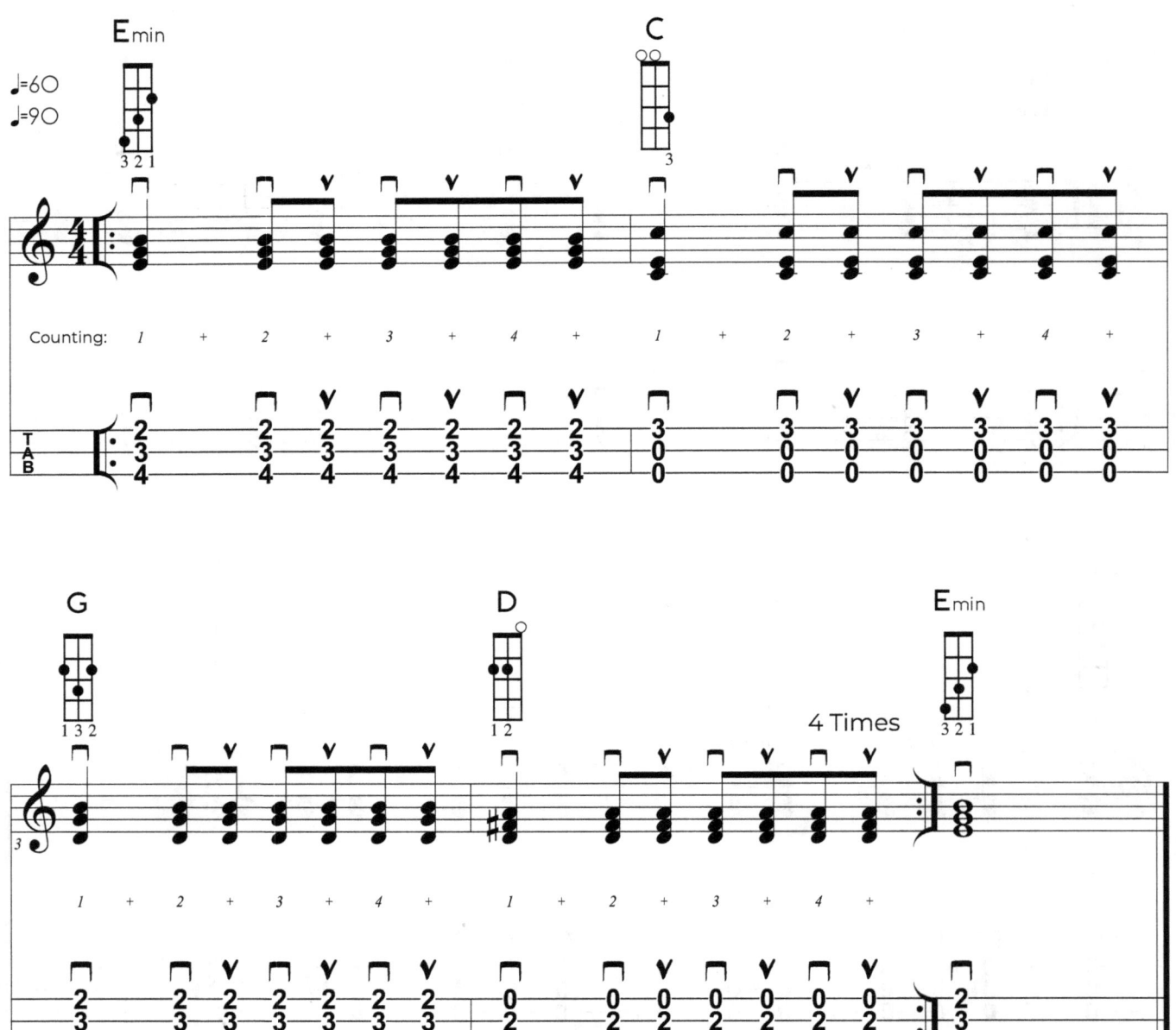

STRUMMING TECHNIQUE #7
C - F - C - G

This lesson uses the "C," "F," and "G" chords. The progression goes from "C" to "F" back to "C" and to "G." The strum pattern is called the granddaddy or island strum. It uses a tie (hold) between the "+ of 2" and beat "3," so don't strum on beat "3." The strum pattern is Down-Down-Up-Up-Down-Up.

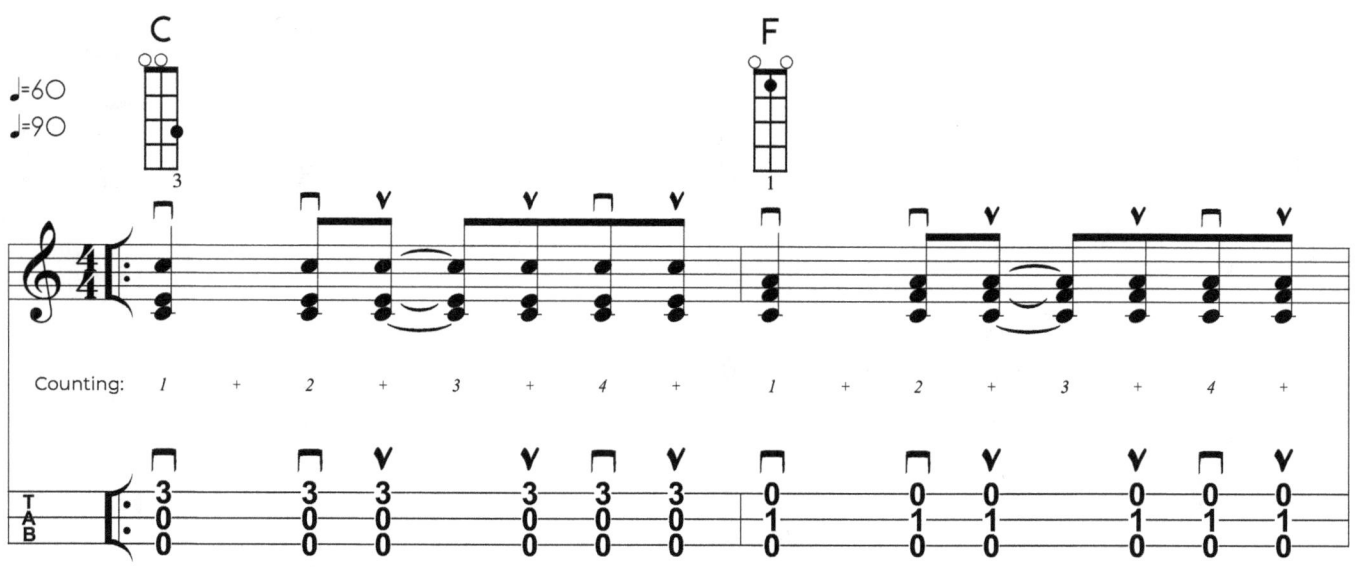

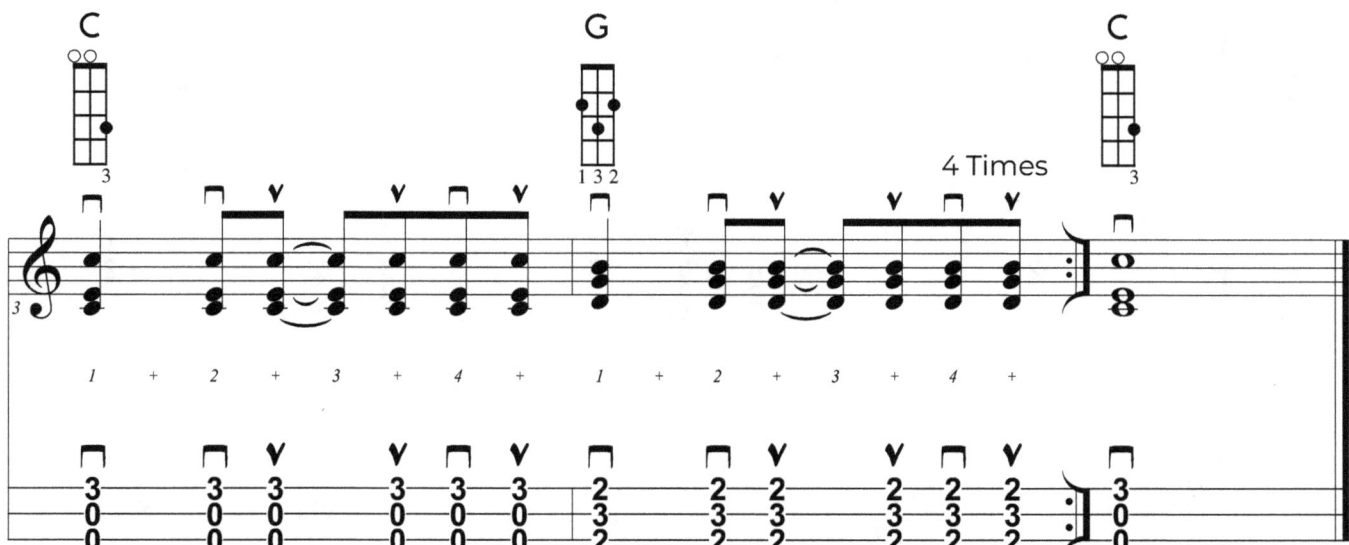

STRUMMING TECHNIQUE #8
Shine On

This lesson has an "A" and "B" section and uses the "G," "D," "Emin," and "C" chords. The "A" section is the classic I – IV – VI – V progression which can be heard in hundreds of songs. The "B" starts on the "Emin" chord and then moves down to the "D," "C," and ends on the tonic chord "G." The strum pattern is your standard Down-Down-Up-Down-Down-Up.

STRUMMING TECHNIQUE #9
C - F - G - Gsus4

This lesson introduces the "Gsus4" chord. The progression is "C," "F," "G," and "Gsus4." It's easy to go from the "G" to the "Gsus4," as you only have to add your pinky finger to the first string, third fret. Sus chords are when you take the third degree of the G chord (B note) and move it up to the fourth degree of the chord (C note).
The strum pattern is called the granddaddy or the island strum.

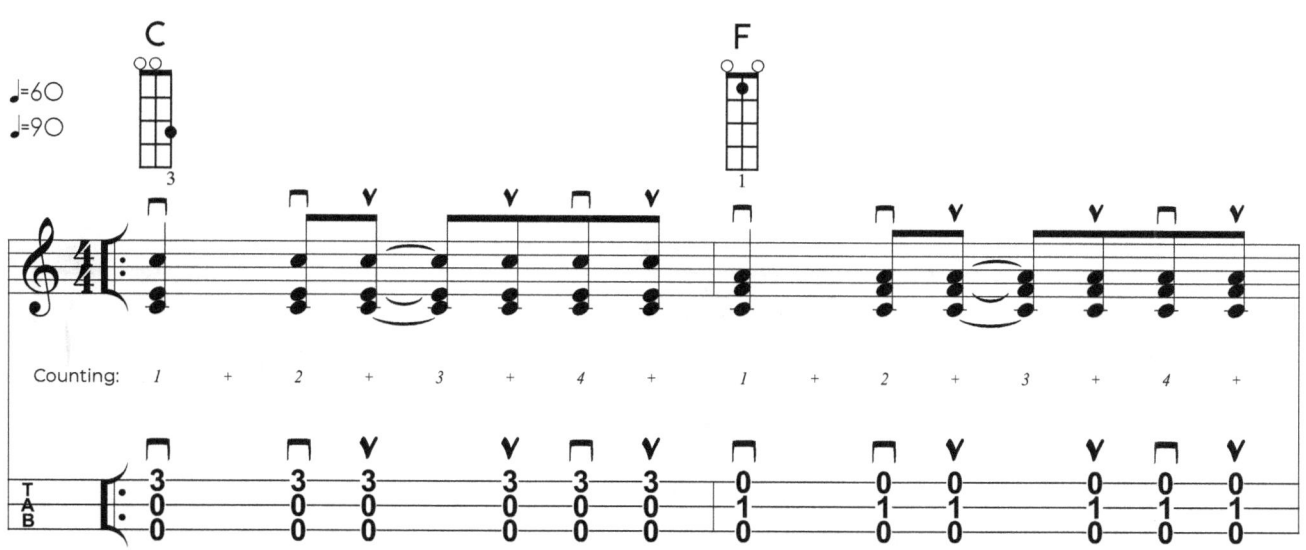

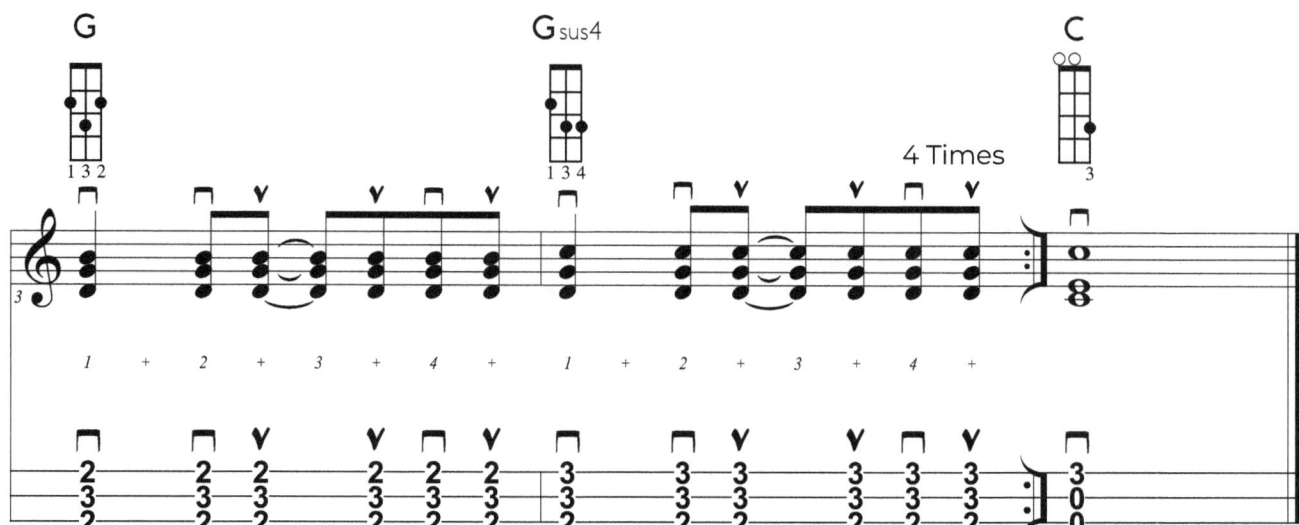

STRUMMING TECHNIQUE #10
C - Csus4 - Bb - Bbsus4

This lesson introduces two new sus chords, the "Csus4" and the "Bbsus4." The progression is "C," "Csus4," "Bb," and "Bbsus4." The "Bb" and "Bbsus4" are bar chords where you use your first or index finger to "bar" or cover both the first and second strings at the first fret. The strum pattern is the island or granddaddy strum.

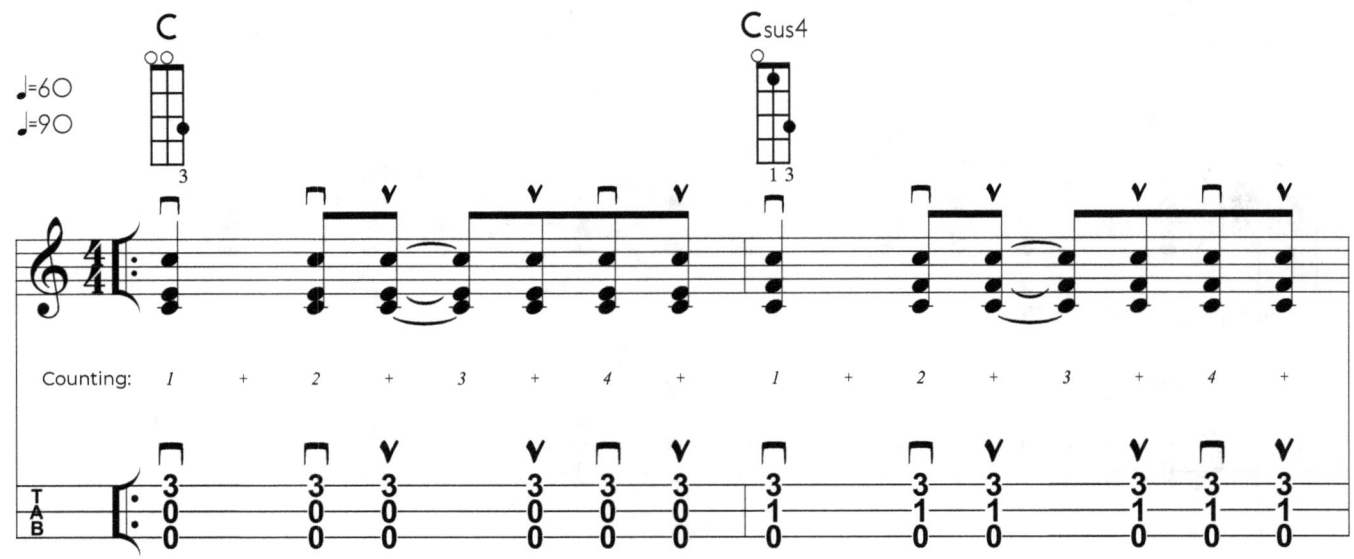

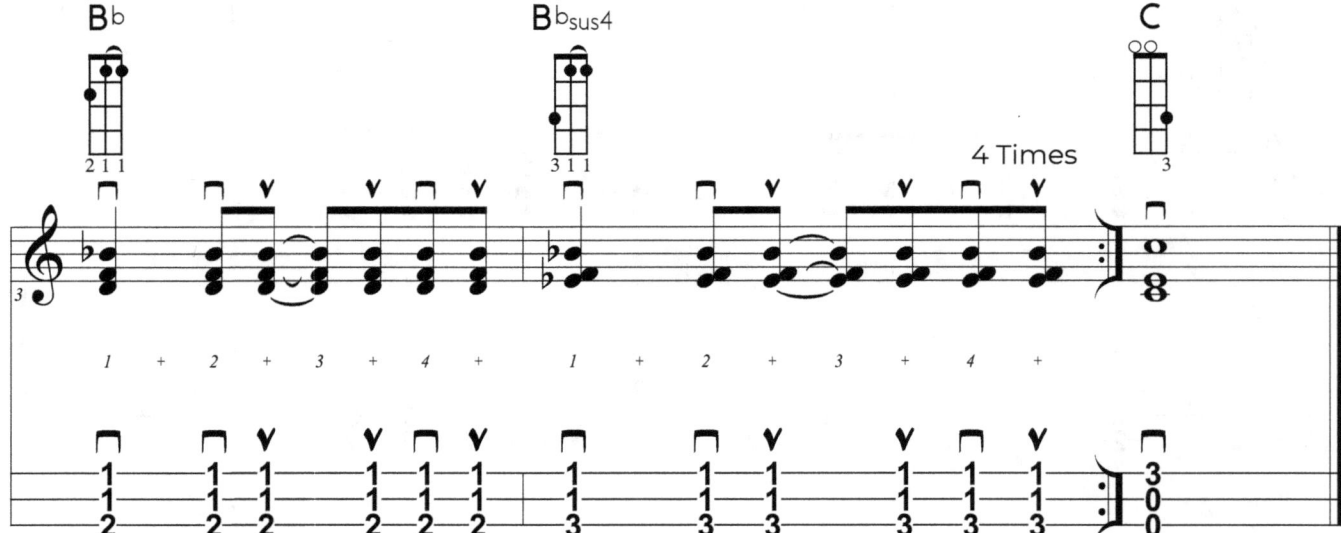

STRUMMING TECHNIQUE #11
Bayliner
PG. 1 of 2

This lesson not only has a great chord progression but adds mutes to the granddaddy strum. You will learn new chords including the "B," "E7," and two "A" chord shapes. The strumming mutes (x), also called "chucks," are on beats "2" and "4," and are done by placing the palm of your strumming hand on the strings right before you strum, creating a muted sound.

STRUMMING TECHNIQUE #11
PG. 2 of 2

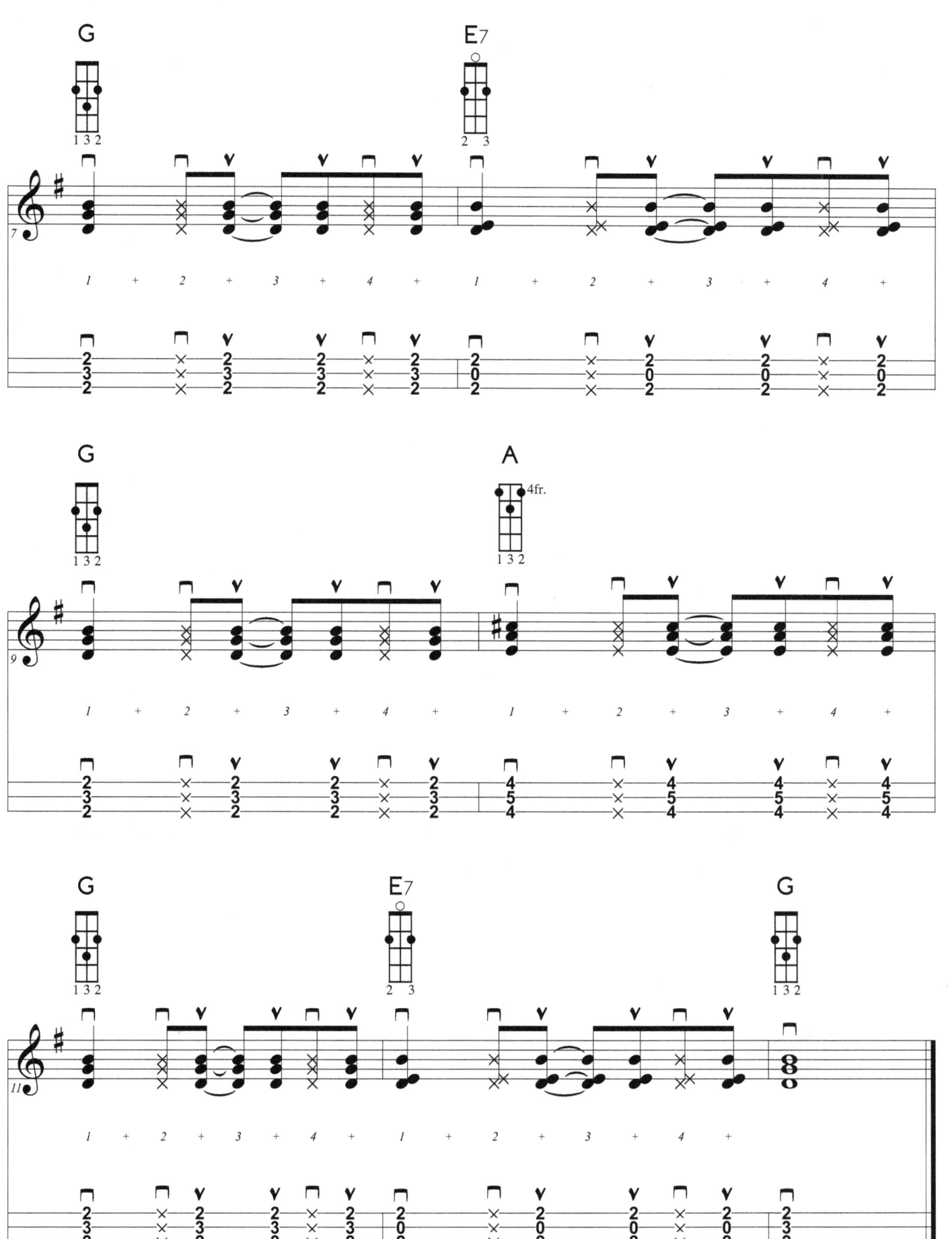

STRUMMING TECHNIQUE #12
I Won't Hesitate

PG. 1 of 2

This lesson takes a simple progression, "C," "G," "Amin," and "F," and plays it two different ways, one with open chords and one with closed chords up the neck. The strum pattern is constant Down-Up eighth notes with palm mutes on beats "2" and "4." Practice both versions until you feel comfortable and confident playing both.

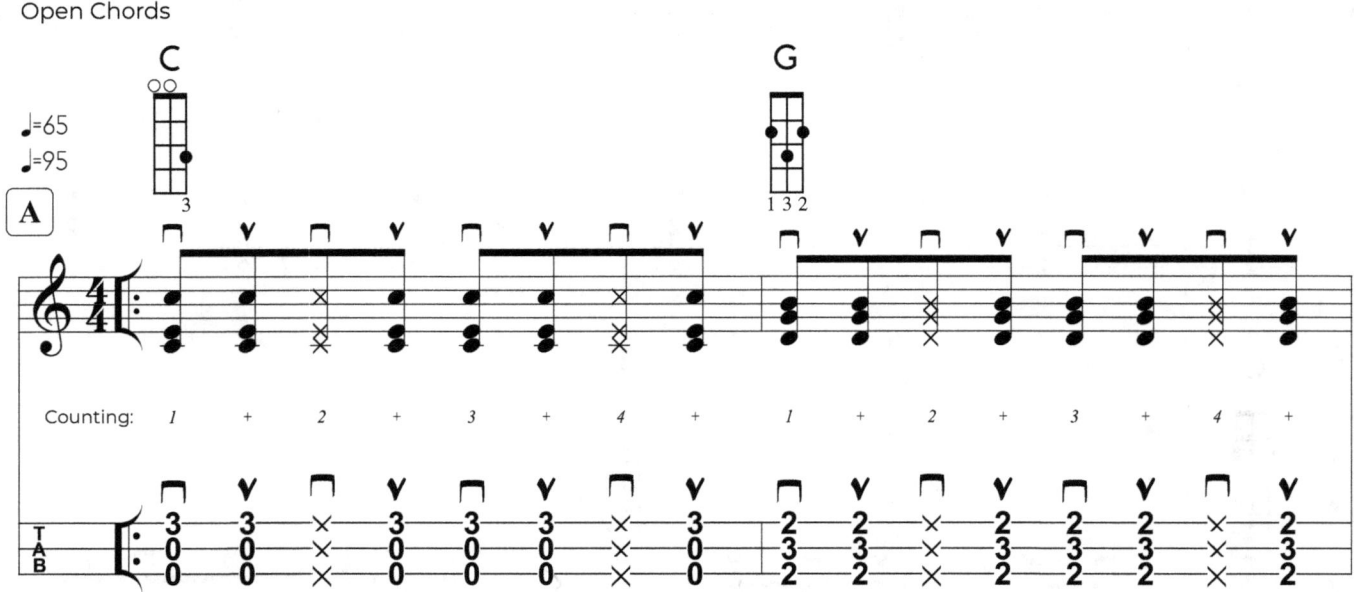

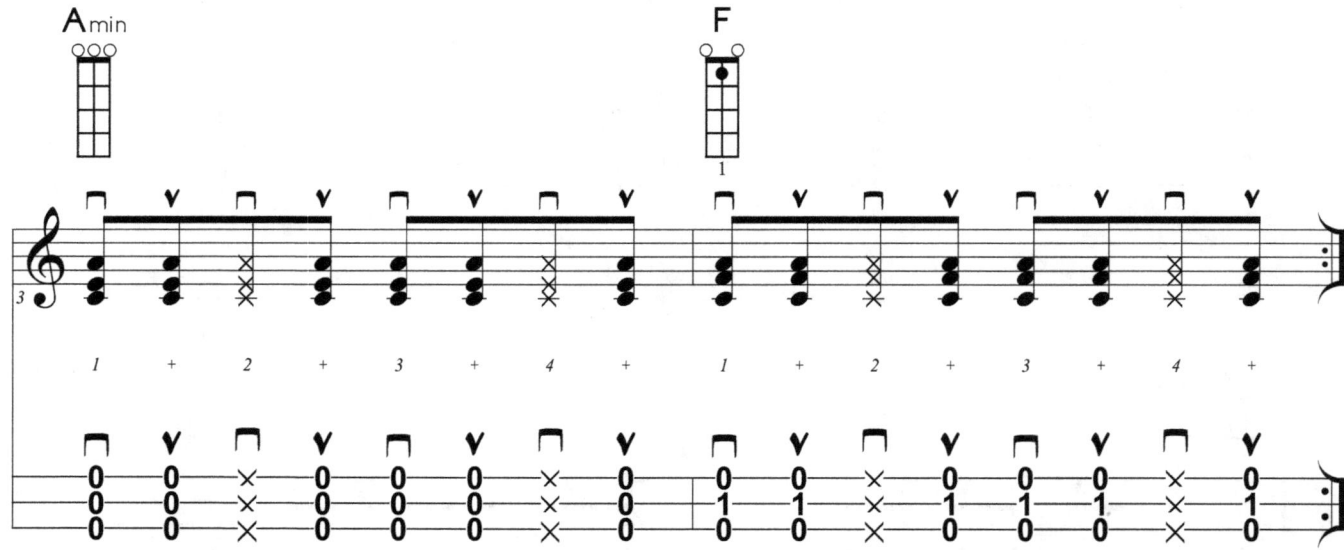

STRUMMING TECHNIQUE #12

Closed Chords

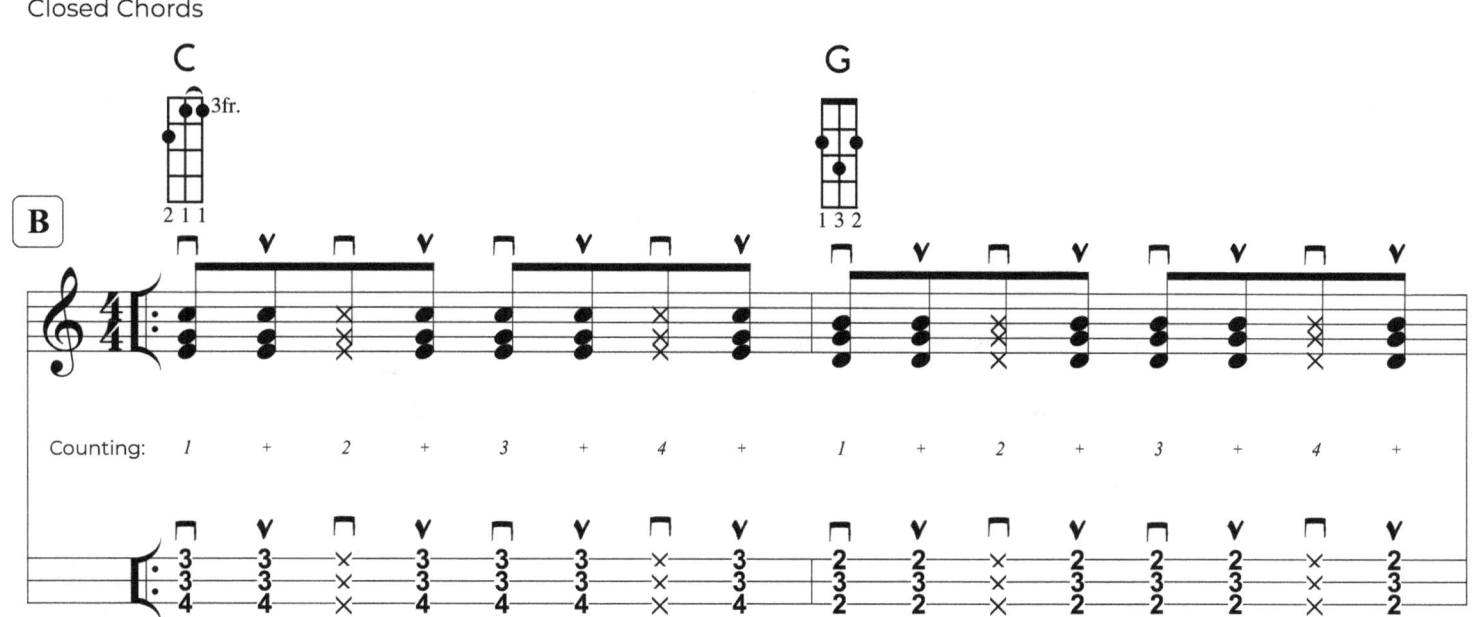

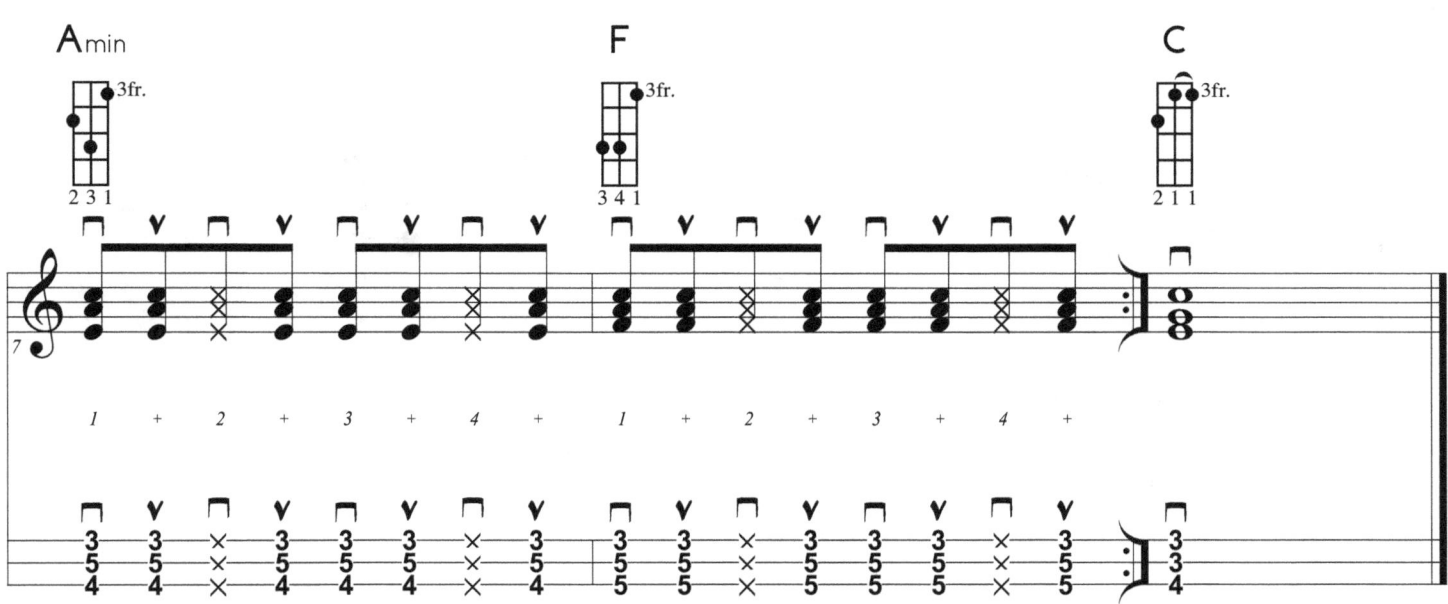

'EKOLU STRUMMING MASTERY
ONLINE COURSE

STRUMMING TECHNIQUE #13
Lemon Drops
PG. 1 of 2

This chord progression can still be heard ringing through the islands of Hawaii. The chords "C," "Emin," "F," "Amin," and "G" are easy, but the way they flow along with the granddaddy strum is beautiful. Both the "A" and the "B" sections will be repeated.

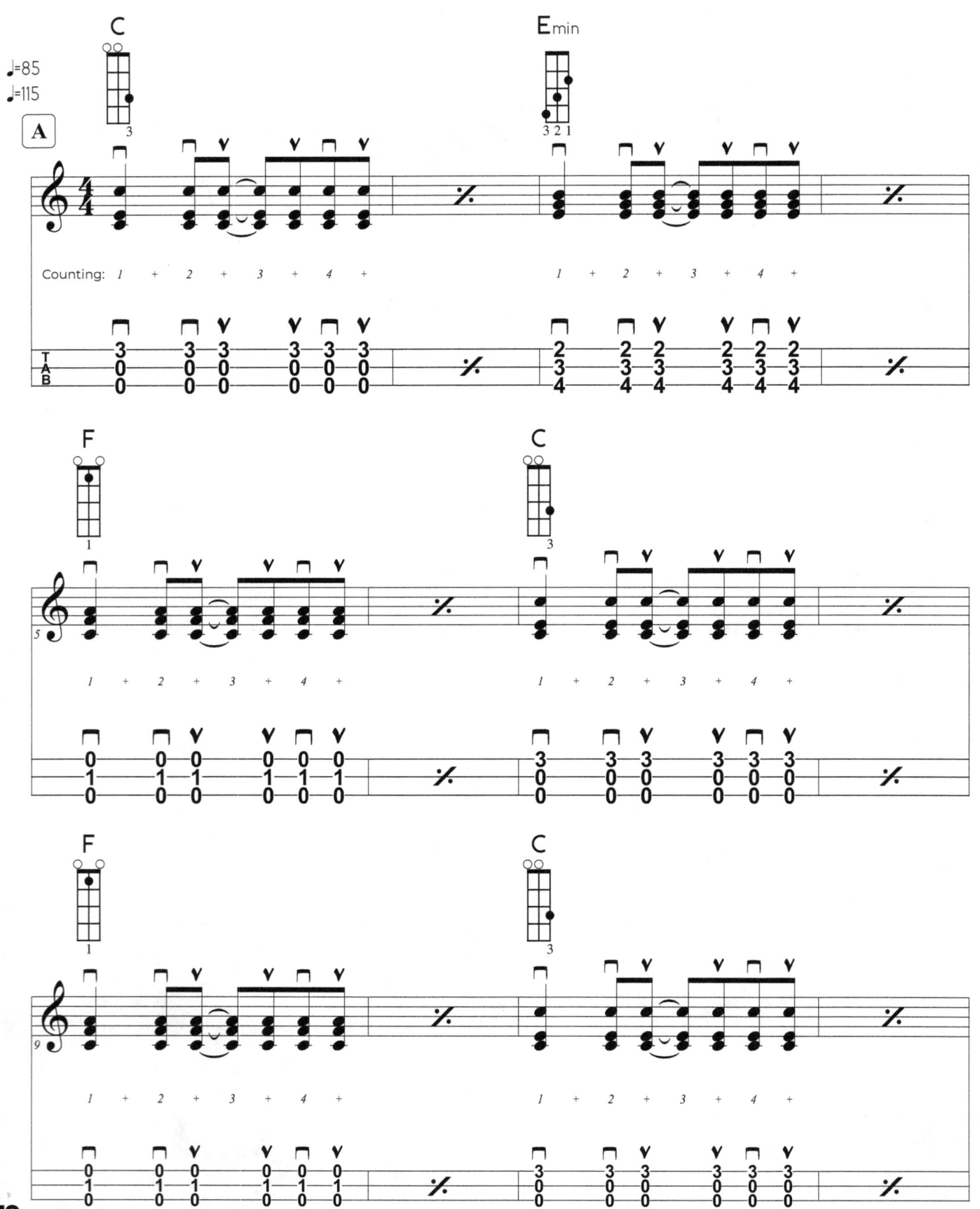

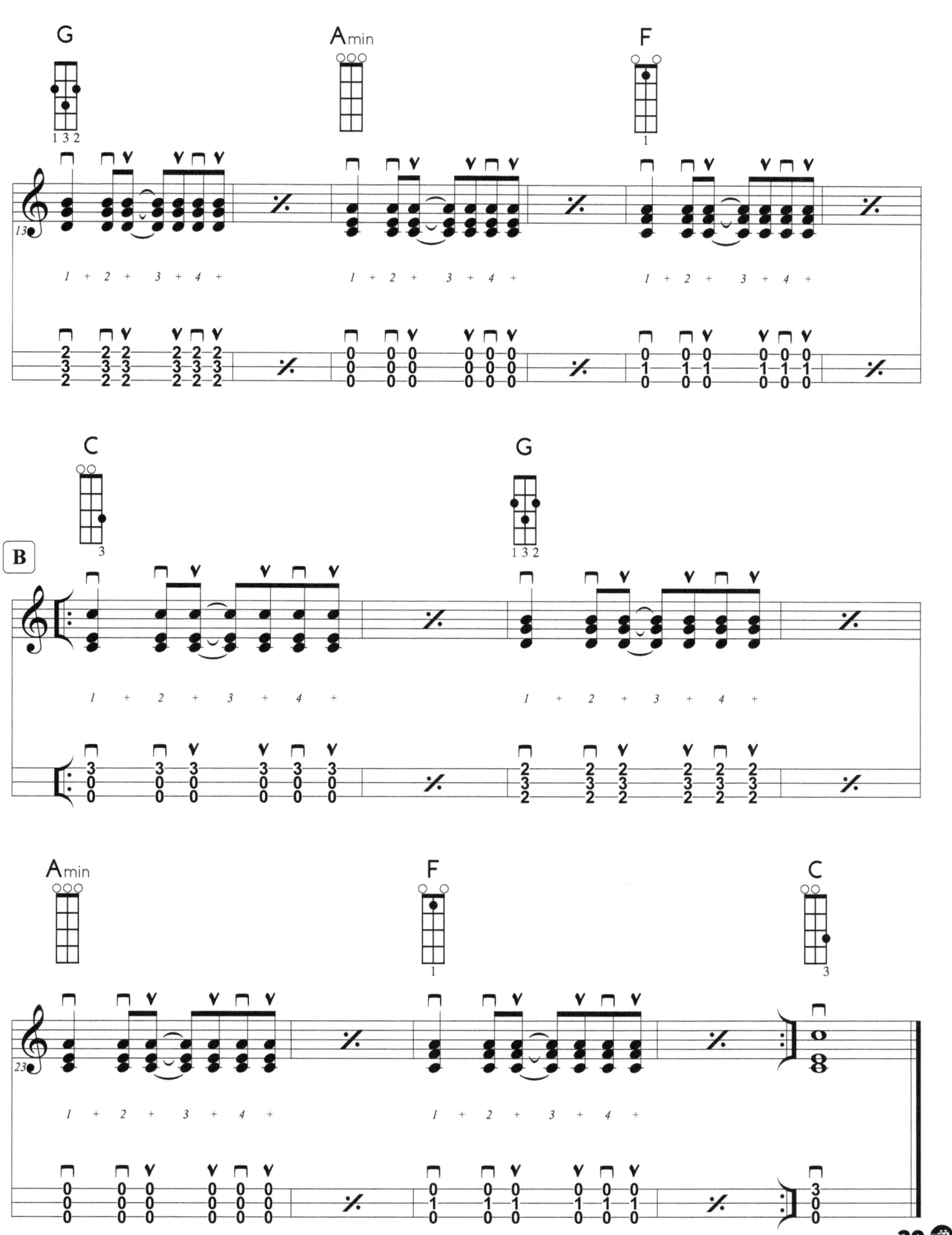

STRUMMING TECHNIQUE #14
Yellow Canary's

This lesson will show how to play a reggae strum pattern. The reggae feel is accomplished by playing up strokes on the "off" beats or the "+" of beats 1, 2, 3, and 4. Even though there are only three chords "A," "D," and "E," they are played with some new shapes that move up to higher frets.

STRUMMING TECHNIQUE #15
Sancho's Revenge

This is another reggae strum pattern that uses a quick Down-Up sixteenth note strum pattern on the "off" beats. The chord progression is unique as it uses the "E," "Ab," "Dbmin," and "B" chords. Each chord is played for one measure and the busier strum pattern creates a funky reggae sound.

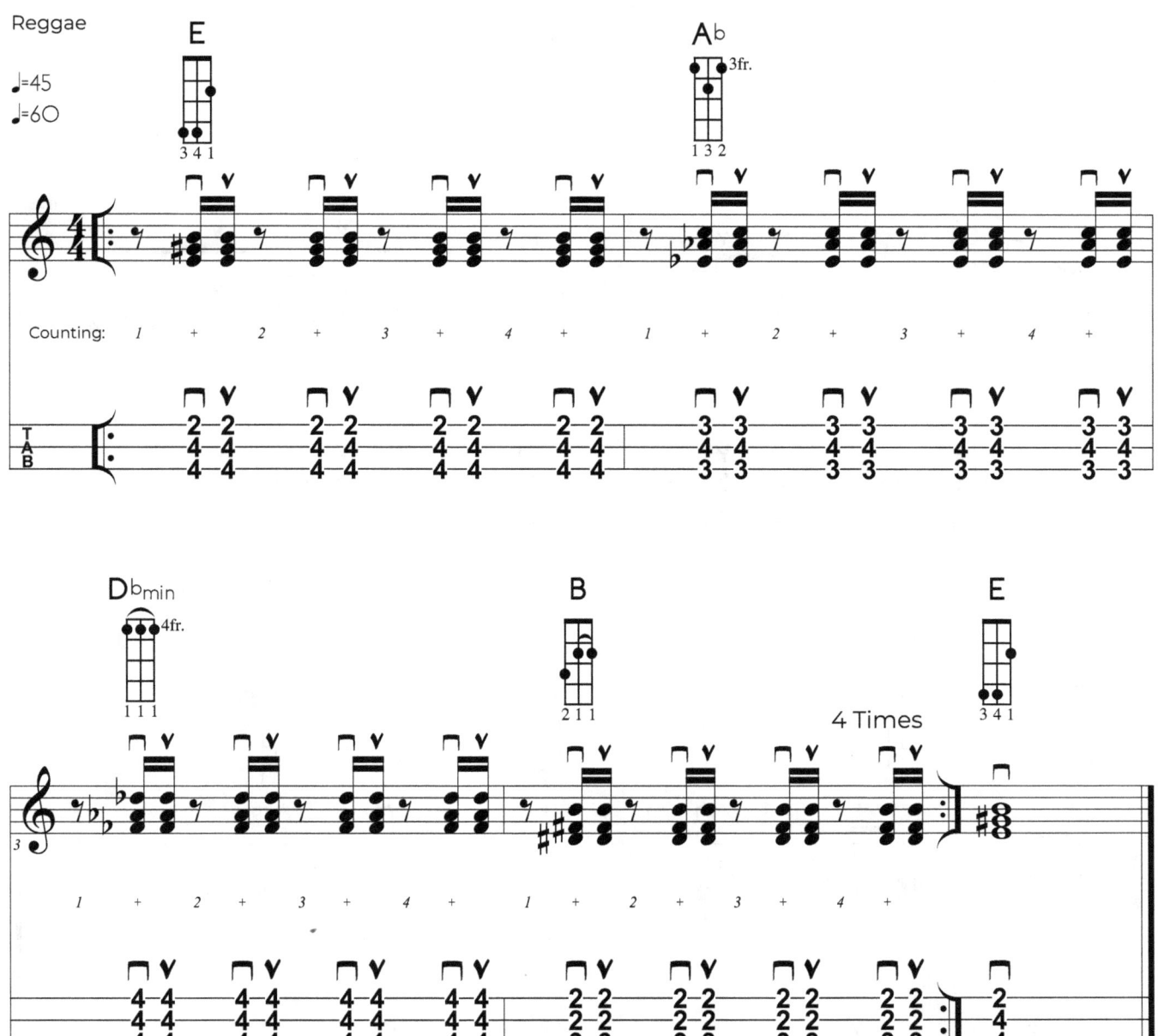

STRUMMING TECHNIQUE #16
Hawaiian VAMP

This lesson shows how to play a Hawaiian vamp that can be used as an intro, outro, and interlude. The progression is II (D7), V (G7), I (C), but it also has a twist with the "Csus4" chord and the classic walk up from "Bb," "B," to "C," heard in many Hawaiian songs.

ALL YOUR MUSIC NEEDS
TERRYCARTERMUSICSTORE.COM

STRUMMING TECHNIQUE #17
Hawaiian Noho Pai Pai

This lesson shows the timeless Hawaiian song "Noho Pai Pai." The "A" section uses the same Hawaiian vamp you learned with the main chords of the song starting at the "B" section. There are several rhythms and strum patterns used throughout this song including the granddaddy strum.

STRUMMING TECHNIQUE #17

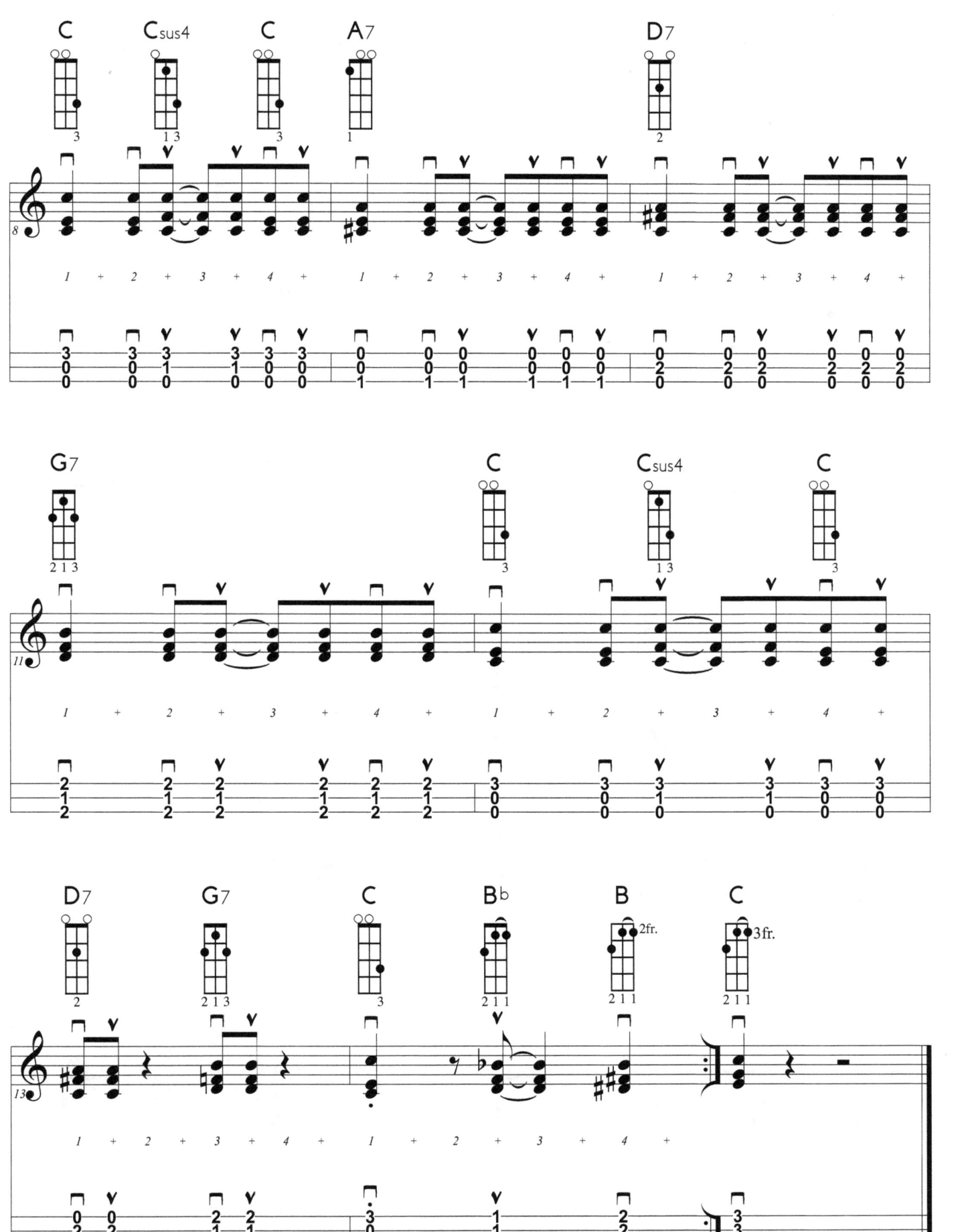

STRUMMING TECHNIQUE #18
Diatonic Chords - C

This lesson shows how to play diatonic chords in the key of "C." The chords will be "C," "Dmin," "Emin," "F," "G," "Amin," and "Bdim." Each chord gets two beats and will use the Down-Down-Up strum pattern. The "A" section ascends up the progression while the "B" section descends back down. Memorize all these chords as you will see them again.

STRUMMING TECHNIQUE #18

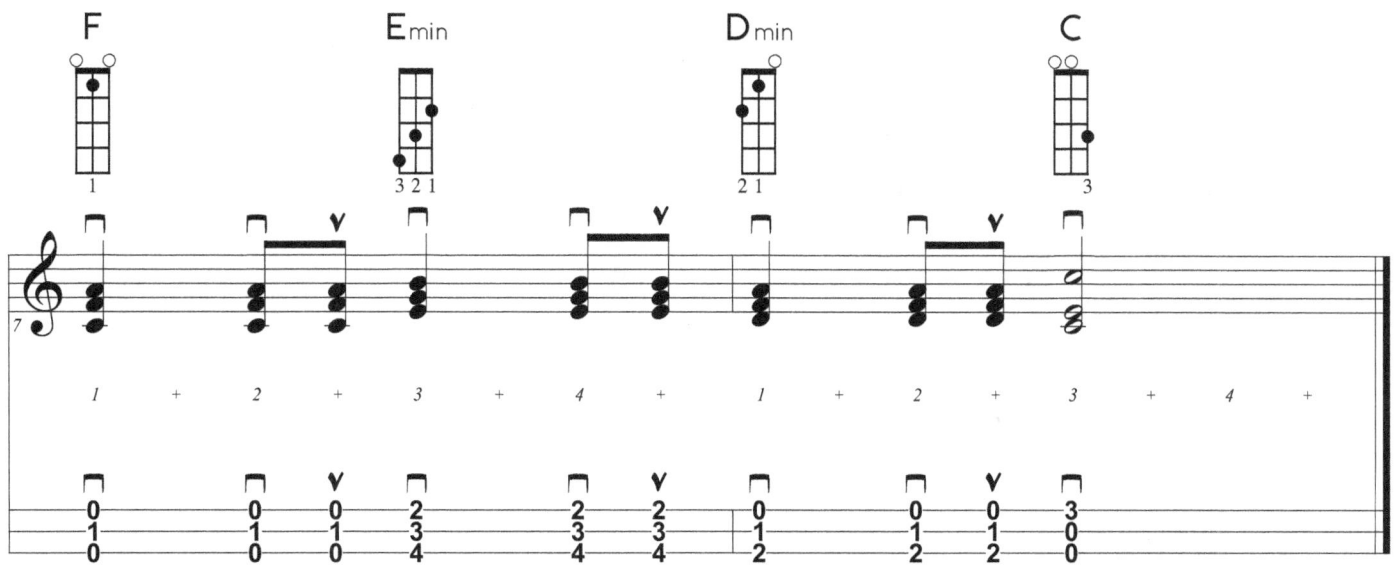

STRUMMING TECHNIQUE #19
Diatonic Chords - G

This lesson shows how to play diatonic chords in the key of "G." The chords will be "G," "Amin," "Bmin," "C," "D," "Emin," and "F#dim." Each chord gets two beats and will use the Down-Down-Up strum pattern. The "A" section ascends up the progression while the "B" section descends back down. Memorize all these chords as you will see them again.

STRUMMING TECHNIQUE #19

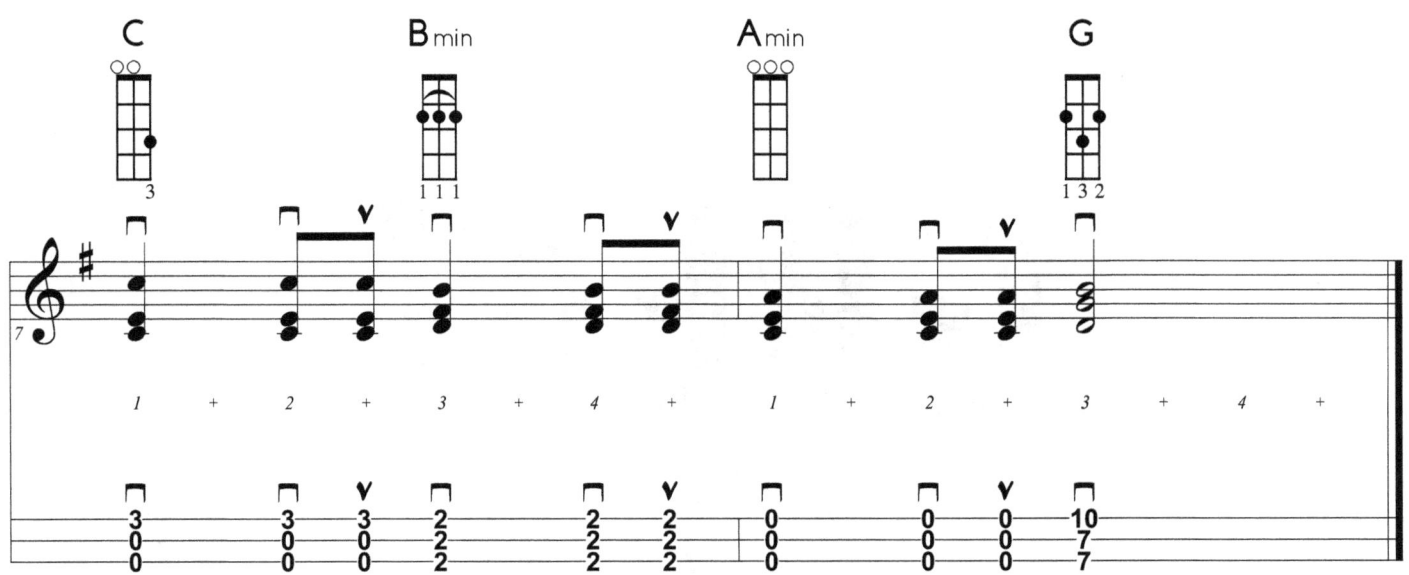

PLATINUM MEMBERSHIP

INCLUDES:

- Early access to all new courses
- FREE Weekly Practice Guide
- All Beginner, Intermediate, And Advanced Courses For Ukulele, Baritone And Guitarlele
- Live Q & A Session: Beginner Ukulele, Intermediate / Advanced Ukulele, Baritone And Guitarlele
- Access to All Workshops
- Access To All Challenges And Giveaways
- ULTP Song Catalog
- Special Discount For ULTP Merch
- Downloadable Backing Tracks
- Downloadable Tab And Music Sheets
- Access To ULTP Community
- Access To ULTP Forum
- Access To ULTP Members Guide
- 30 Day 100% Money Back Guarantee.

GREAT JOB!

I want to congratulate you for getting through the Uke Like The Pros 'Ekolu Ukulele Strumming Mastery Book. I am proud of you for making the commitment to yourself and your playing. You should now have a better understanding of the 'Ekolu, be a more skilled ukulele player, play with better timing, and feel more confident in your abilities.

Now that you are a 'Ekolu Ukulele Master, it's time for you to take the next step in your playing by signing up for a FREE Month of the Platinum Membership. Platinum Members have access to over 30 Courses, Challenges, Giveaways, Workshops, and LIVE Q&A sessions with our members.

Get your FREE Membership:

THE ESSENTIALS

It is important to learn and memorize these terms and symbols because they not only apply to ukulele but to all music.

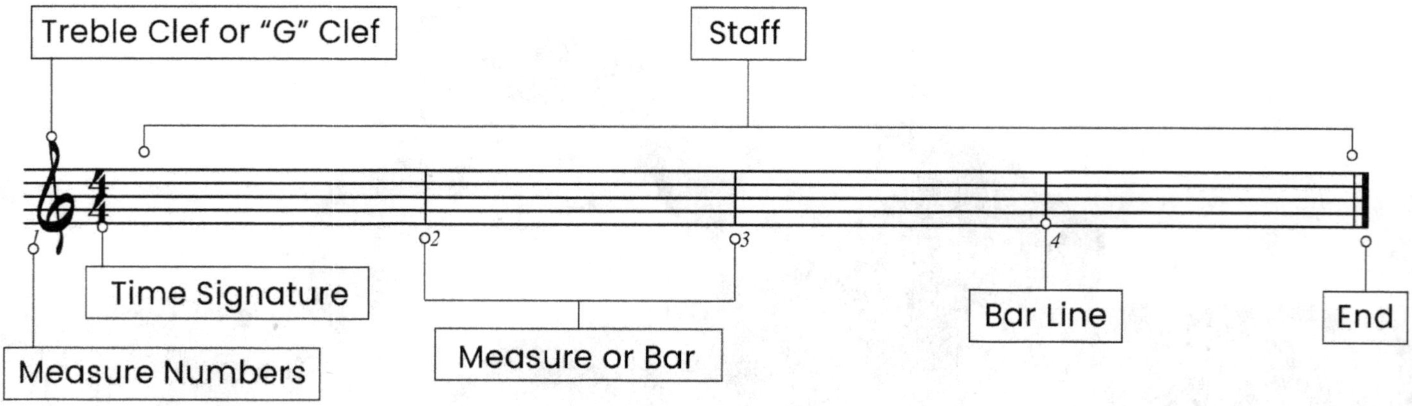

- Treble Clef or "G" Clef
- Staff
- Time Signature
- Measure Numbers
- Measure or Bar
- Bar Line
- End

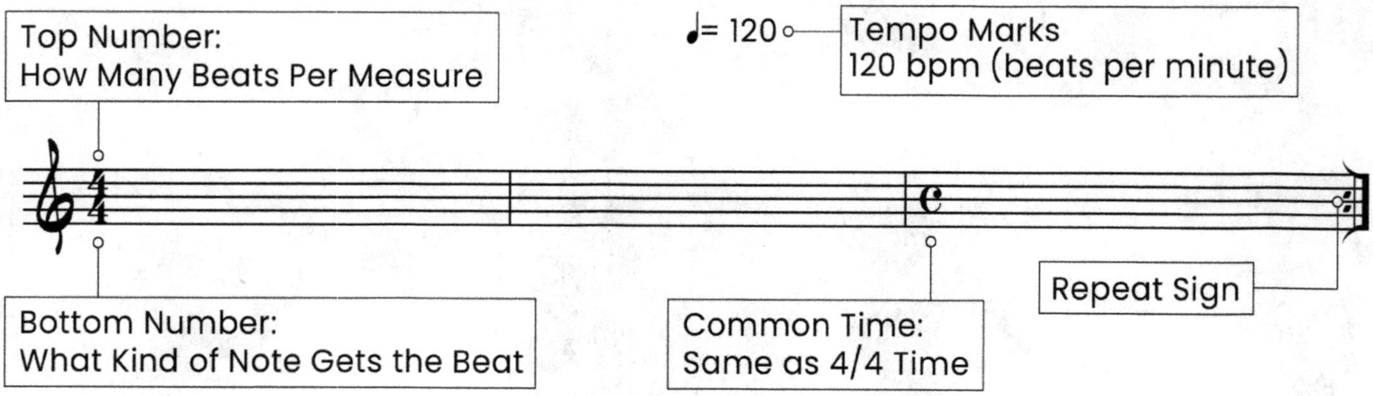

- Top Number: How Many Beats Per Measure
- Tempo Marks ♩= 120 bpm (beats per minute)
- Bottom Number: What Kind of Note Gets the Beat
- Common Time: Same as 4/4 Time
- Repeat Sign

Notes On The Staff: There are seven notes in music (A, B, C, D, E, F, G) and they move up and down alphabetically on the staff.

G A B C D E F G A B C D E F G A B C D E F

How To Remember The Notes:

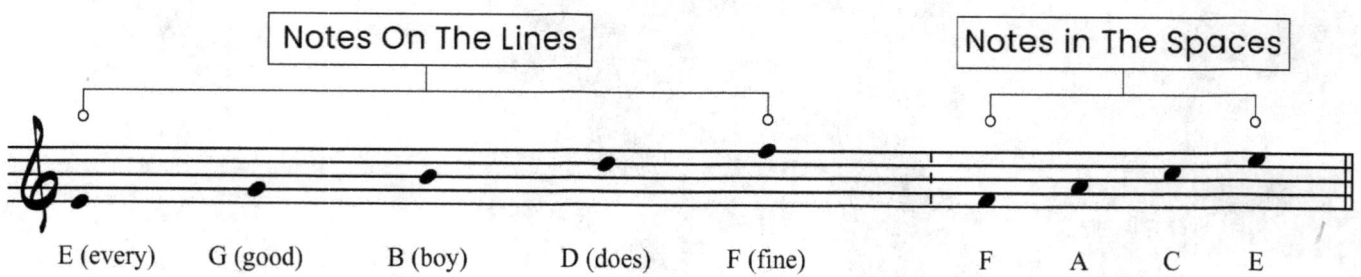

Notes On The Lines: E (every)   G (good)   B (boy)   D (does)   F (fine)

Notes in The Spaces: F   A   C   E

A

HOW TO READ TAB

Tablature (TAB) is a form of music reading for 'Ekolu Ukulele that uses a 3 line TAB staff and numbers. Each line of the staff represents a string on the 'Ekolu Ukulele and the numbers represent which fret you play on. When looking at the TAB staff it reads like it's upside down on the paper compared to the strings of your 'Ekolu Ukulele. On the TAB staff, the highest line (closest to the sky) represents the 1st string (A string) of the ukulele, while the lowest line (closest to the ground) represents the 3rd string (C string) of the 'Ekolu Ukulele. When you see 2 or more notes stacked on top of each other on the TAB staff, that means you play those notes at the same time, like a chord.

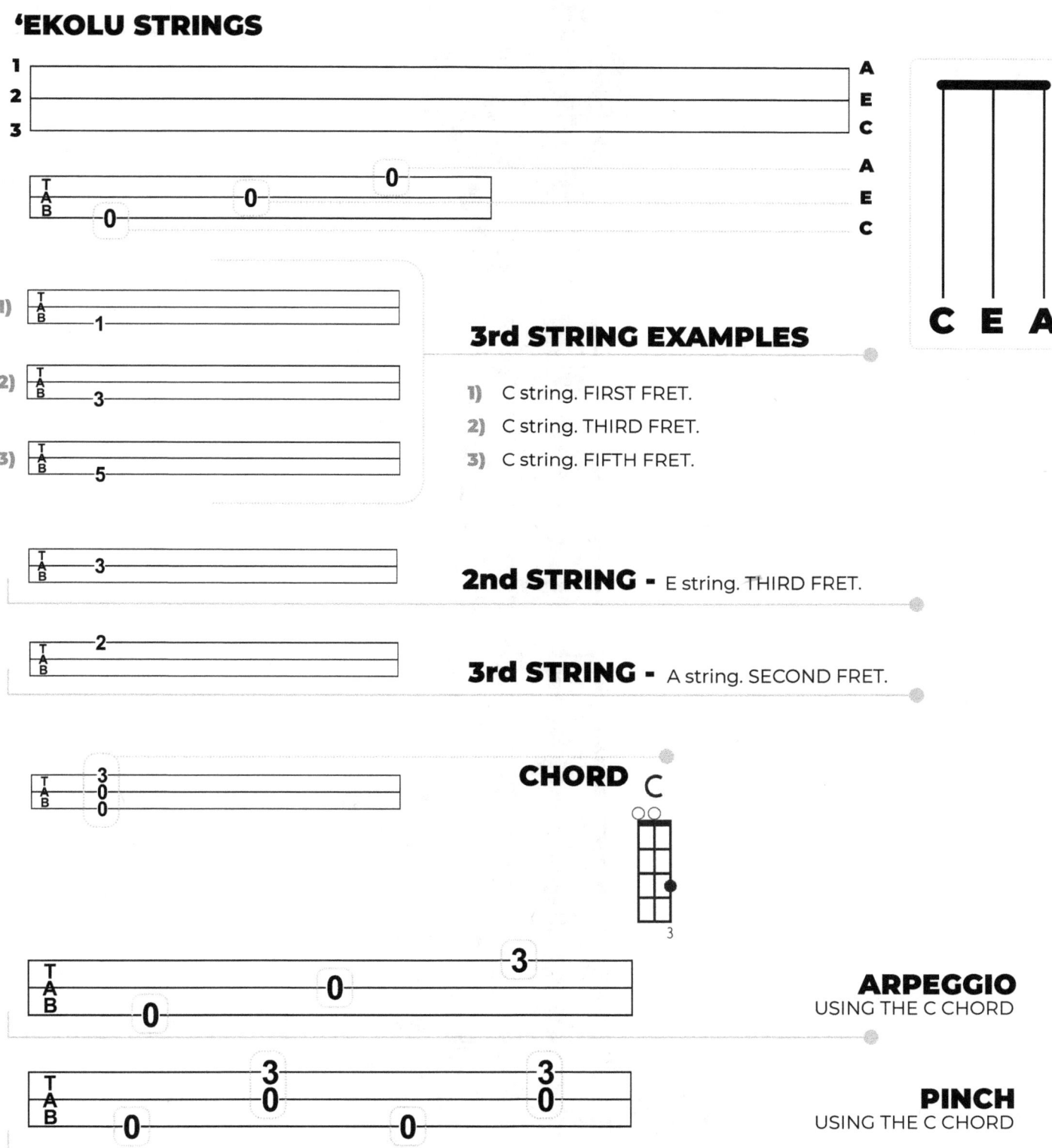

NOTES ON THE 'EKOLU NECK

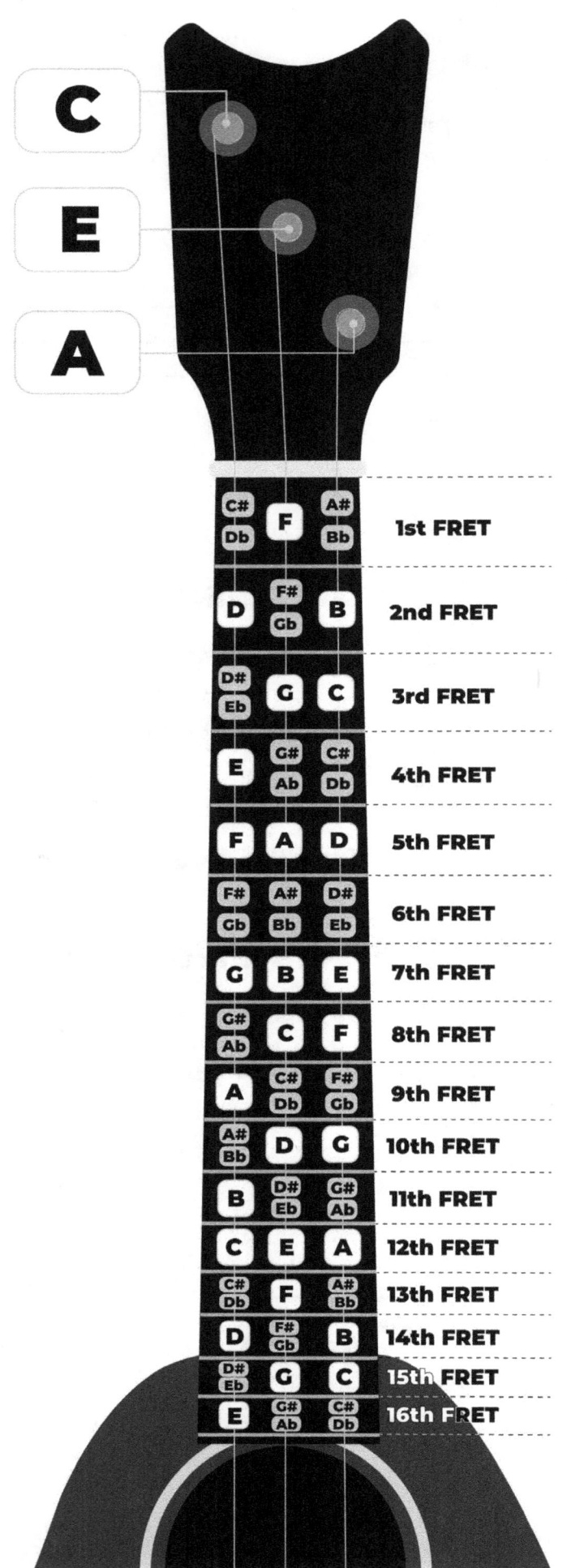

ʻEKOLU HANDS

When playing fingerstyle on your ʻekolu ukulele, you will see both letters and numbers to indicate which fingers to use both for picking hand and your fretting hand. These letters and numbers will show up in the music notation, TAB, and chord diagrams.

FRETTING HAND	PICKING HAND
The left hand for right-handed players. will be indicated in the music or chord diagrams by numbers: **1**=Index finger **3**=Ring finger **2**=Middle finger **4**=Pinky finger	The right hand for right-handed players. will be indicated in the music by letters: **p**=Thumb **m**= Middle **i**= Index

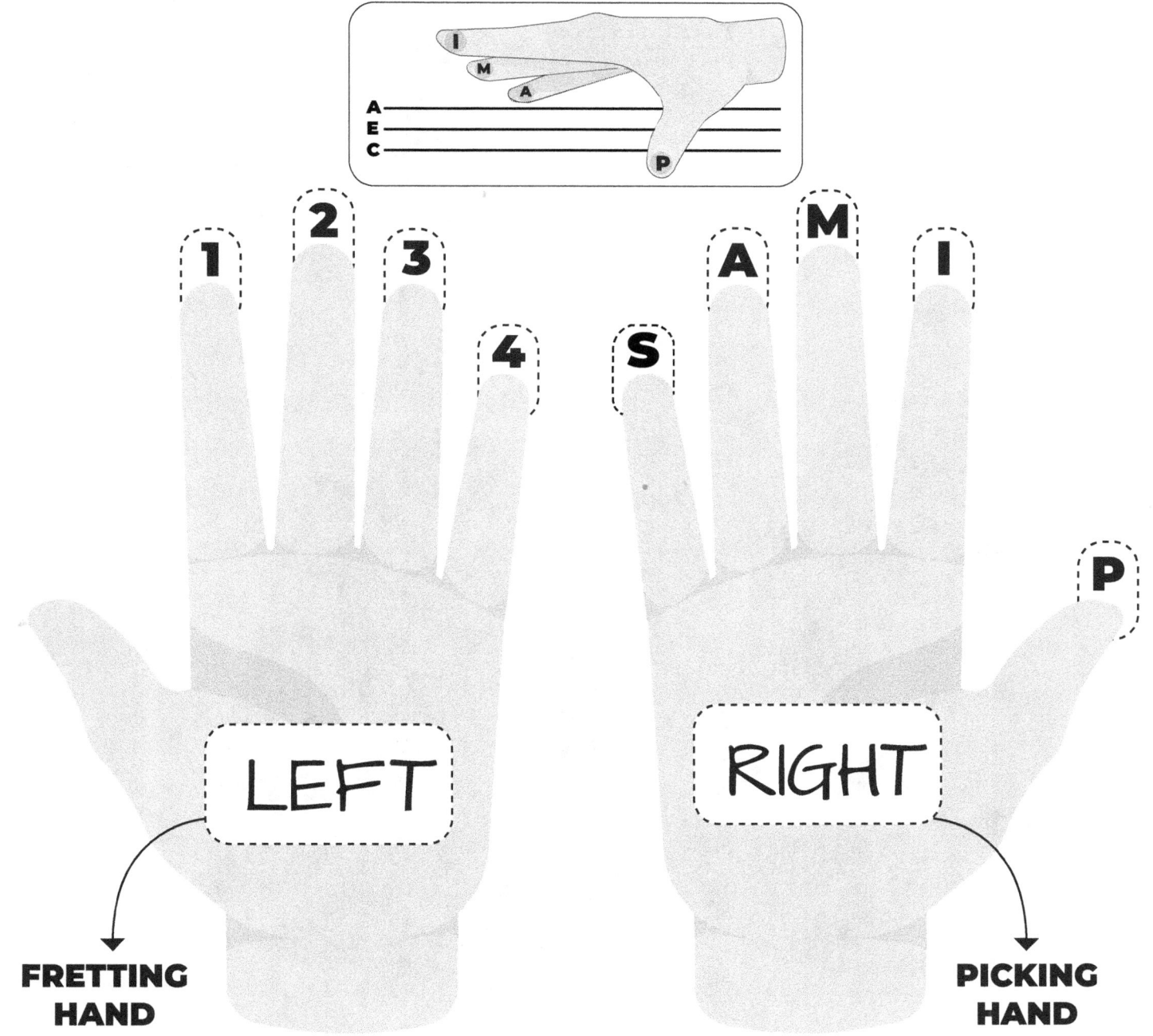

'EKOLU UKULELE PARTS

UNDERSTANDING 'EKOLU CHORD DIAGRAMS

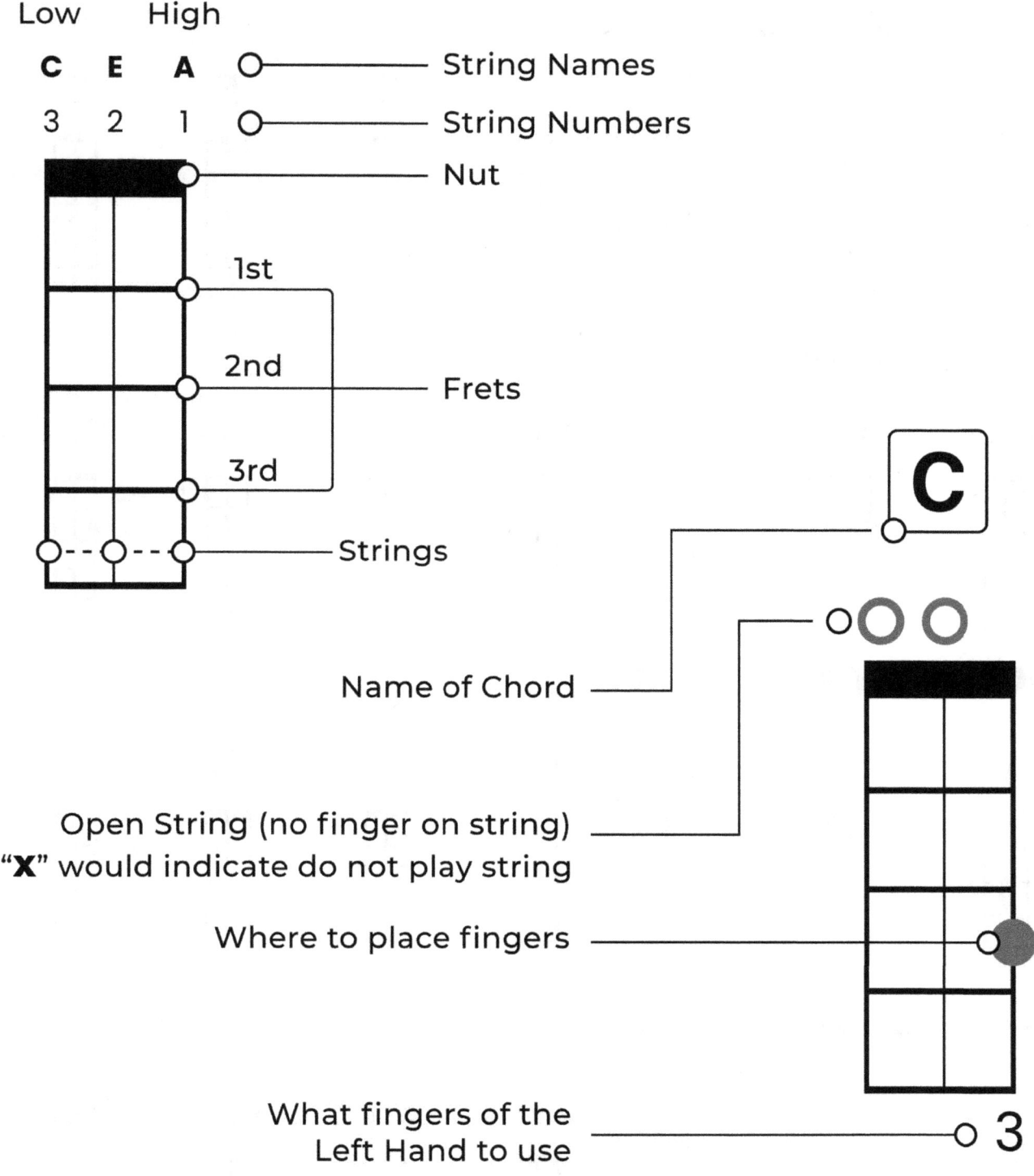

'EKOLU CHORD CHART

When playing fingerstyle on your 'Ekolu Ukulele, you will see both letters and numbers to indicate which fingers to use both for picking hand and your fretting hand. These letters and numbers will show up in the music notation, TAB, and chord diagrams.

MAJOR CHORDS

A	B	C	D	E	F	G
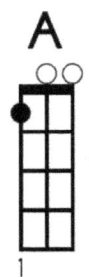	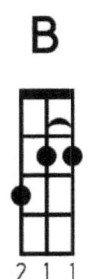		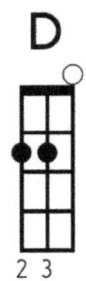	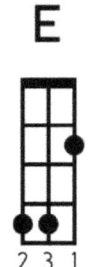	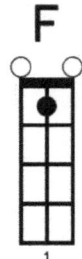	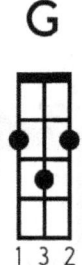

MINOR CHORDS

Amin	Bmin	Cmin	Dmin	Emin	Fmin	Gmin
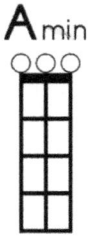			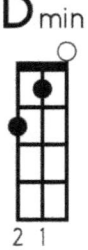	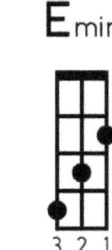	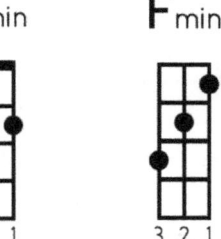	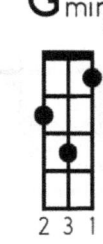

DOMINANT 7TH CHORDS

A7	B7	C7	D7	E7	F7	G7
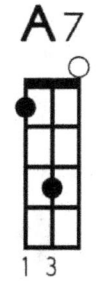	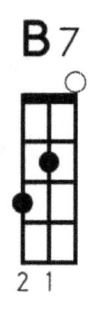	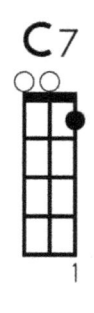	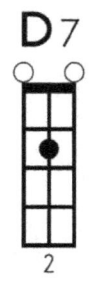	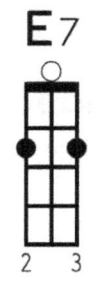	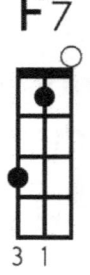	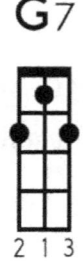

SUS CHORDS

Asus4	Bsus4	Csus4	Dsus4	Esus4	Fsus4	Gsus4
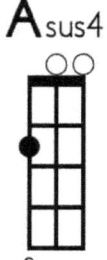	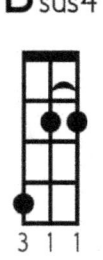	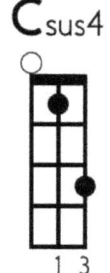	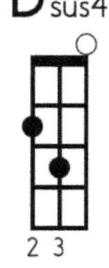	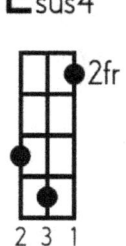	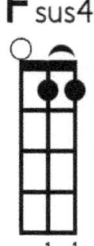	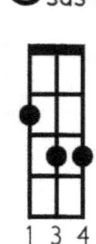

MAJOR 7TH CHORDS

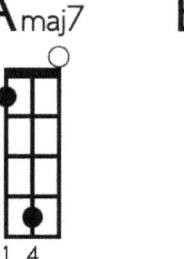 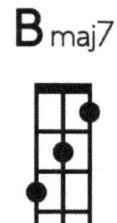 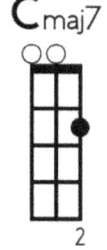    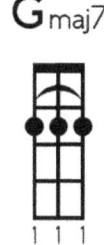

MINOR 7TH CHORDS

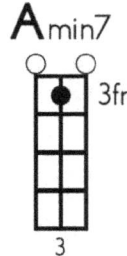 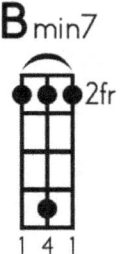 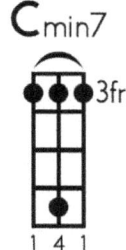 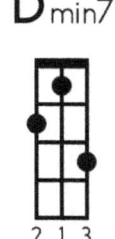 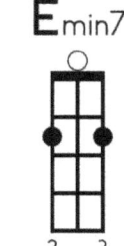 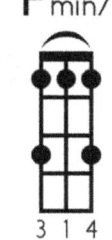 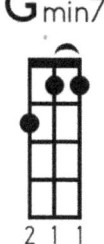

DIMINISHED CHORDS

 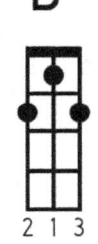 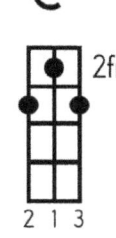 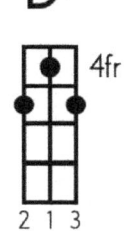 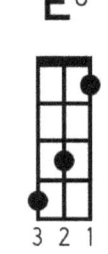 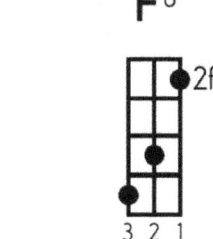

AUGMENTED CHORDS

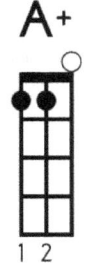 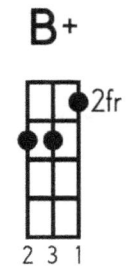 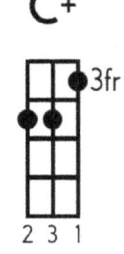 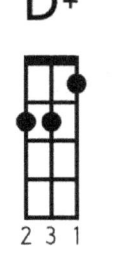 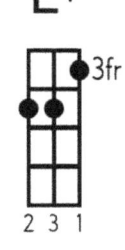 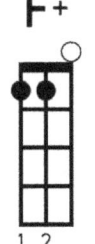 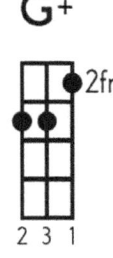

COOL CHORDS

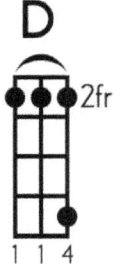 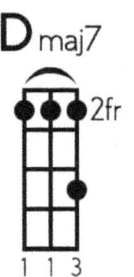   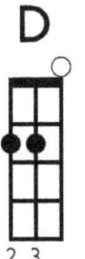 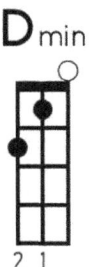

MUSIC SYMBOLS TO KNOW - 'EKOLU

A variety of symbols, articulations, repeats, hammer on's, pull off's, bends, and slides.

D.C. al Fine — *D.C.* (da capo) means go to the beginning of the tune and stop when you get to **Fine**

D.C. al Coda — *D.C.* means go to the beginning of the tune and jump to *Coda* ⊕ when you see this sign ⊕

D.S. al Fine — *D.S.* (dal segno) means go to the *Sign* 𝄋 and stop when you get to **Fine**

D.S. al Coda — *D.S.* means go to the *Sign* 𝄋 and jump to the *Coda* ⊕ when you see ⊕

Sim... — Play the same rhythm, strum pattern, or picking pattern as the previous measure

Etc... — Continue the same rhythm, strum pattern, or picking pattern as the previous measure

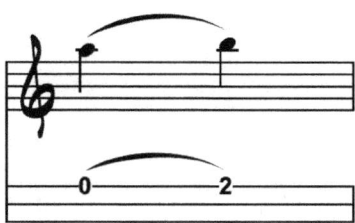

Hammer On:
Pick first note then hammer on to the next note without picking it.

Pull Off:
Pick first note then pull off to the next note without picking it.

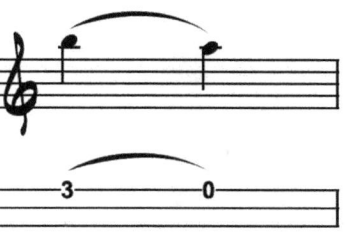

Hammer On & Pull Off:
Pick first note, hammer on to the next note and pull off to the last note all in one motion.

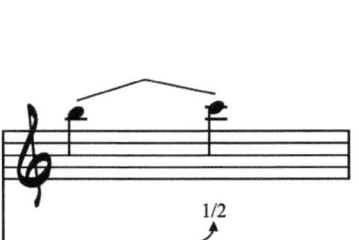

1/2 Step Bend:
Bend the first note a 1/2 step or 1 fret.

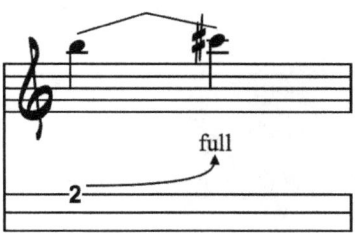

Whole Step Bend:
Bend the first note a whole step or 2 frets.

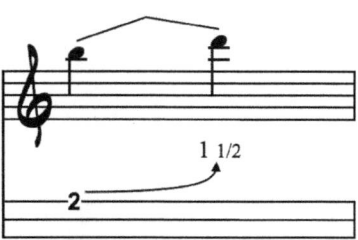

Step & 1/2 Bend:
Bend the first note 1 1/2 steps or 3 frets.

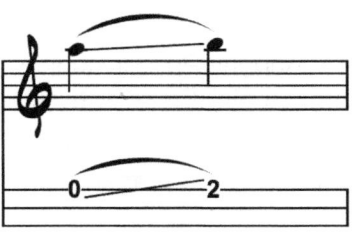

Forward Slide:
Pick first note and slide up to higher note.

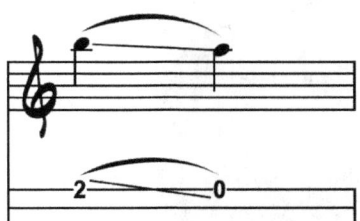

Backward Slide:
Pick first note and slide back to lower note.

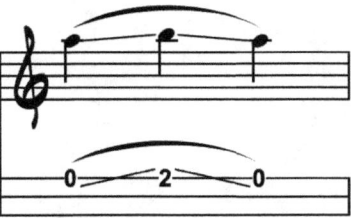

Forward/Backward Slide:
Pick first note, slide up to next note and then slide back.

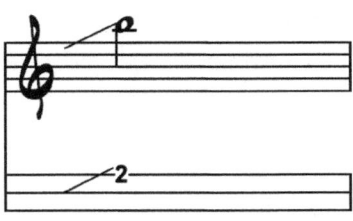

Slide Into Note:
Slide from 2-3 frets below note

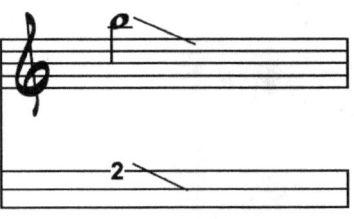

Slide Off Note:
Slide off 2-3 frets after note

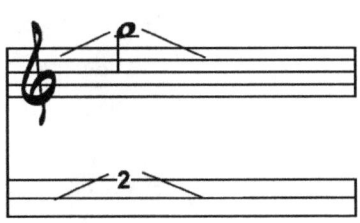

Slide Into Note then Slide Off Note

ABOUT THE AUTHOR

Terry Carter is a San Diego-based ukulele player, surfer, songwriter, and creator of ukelikethepros.com, rocklikethepros.com and terrycartermusicstore.com. With over 30 years as a professional musician, educator and Los Angeles studio musician, Terry has worked with greats like Weezer, Josh Groban, Robby Krieger (The Doors), 2-time Grammy winning composer Christopher Tin (Calling All Dawns), Duff McKagan (Guns N' Roses), Grammy winning producer Charles Goodan (Santana/Rolling Stones), and the Los Angeles Philharmonic. Terry has written and produced tracks for commercials (Discount Tire and Puma) and TV shows, including Scorpion (CBS), Pit Bulls & Parolees (Animal Planet), Trippin', Wildboyz, and The Real World (MTV). He has self-published over 25 books for Uke Like The Pros and Rock Like The Pros, filmed over 30 ukulele and guitar online courses, and has millions of views on his social media channels. Terry received a Master of Music in Studio/Jazz Guitar Performance from University of Southern California and a Bachelor of Music from San Diego State University, with an emphasis in Jazz Studies and Music Education. He has taught at the University of Southern California, San Diego State University, Santa Monica College, Miracosta College, and Los Angeles Trade Tech College.

ONLINE UKULELE COURSES
The perfect place to learn how to play Ukulele, Baritone Ukulele, Guitar and Guitarlele.

ULTP Roadmap
WHERE TO START?

1) UKULELE BEGINNER
A. Beginning Ukulele Starter Course
B. Beginning Ukulele Bootcamp Course
C. Ukulele Fundamentals Course
D. Ukulele Practice & Technique Course
E. Master the Ukulele 1

2) UKULELE INTERMEDIATE
A. Master The Ukulele 2
B. Beginning Music Reading
C. 23 Ultimate Chord Progressions
D. Beginning Ukulele Fingerstyle Course

3) UKULELE ADVANCED
A. Ukulele Blues Mastery Course
B. Beginning Ukulele Soloing Course
C. Fingerstyle Mastery Course
D. Jazz Swing Mastery Course

MORE OPTIONS!

FUNLAND
A. Beginning Ukulele Kids Course Songbook
B. 21 Popular Songs for Ukulele
C. The Best Ukulele Christmas Songs
D. 10 Classic Rock Licks
E. Guitar Fundamentals

BARITONE UKULELE
A. Beginning Baritone Ukulele Bootcamp Course
B. 6 Weeks Baritone Q&A
C. Baritone Blues Mastery Course
D. Beginning Baritone Fingerstyle Course

GUITARLELE
A. Guitarlele Starter Course
B. 6 Weeks Guitarlele Q&A
C. Guitarlele Course for Ukulele and Guitar Players
D. Guitarlele Blues Mastery Course

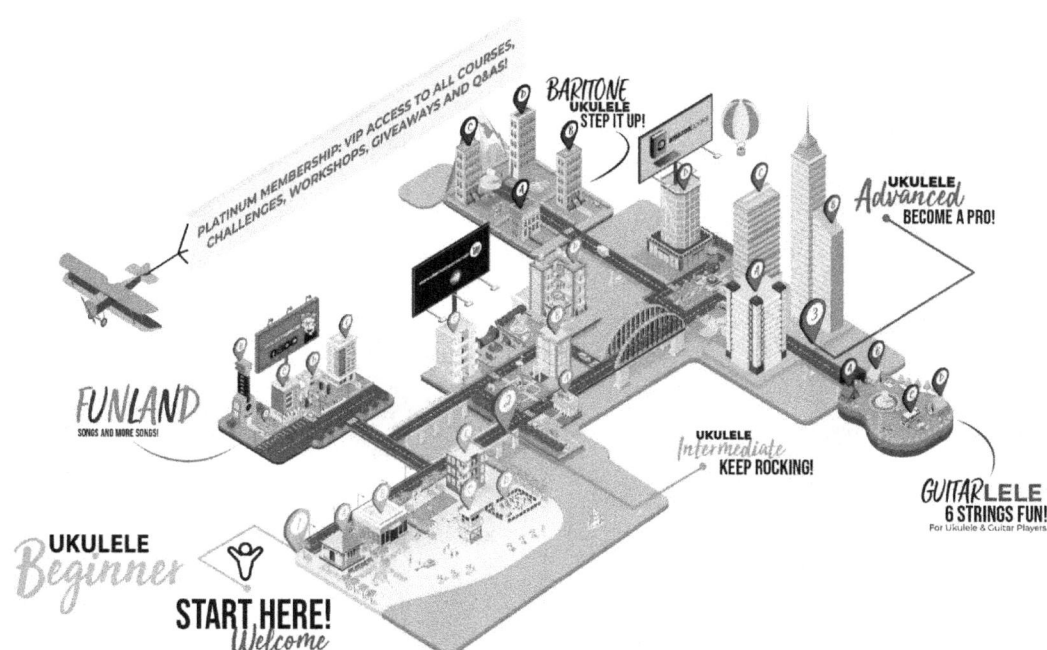

Courses For All Levels
UKELIKETHEPROS.COM

TERRY CARTER MUSIC STORE

All your music needs at the #1 music store, **terrycartermusicstore.com**

'Ekolus

Ukuleles

Guitars

Pro Audio

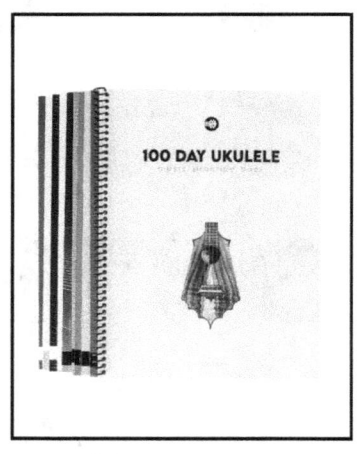

Books

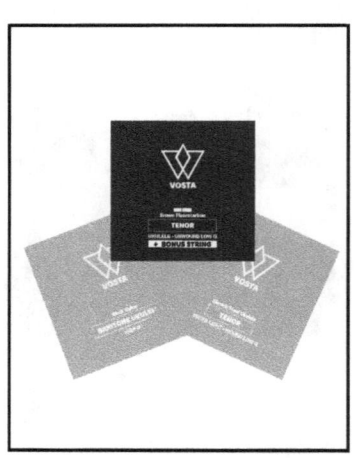

Vosta Strings

UKELIKETHEPROS.COM
BLOG.UKELIKETHEPROS.COM
TERRYCARTERMUSICSTORE.COM
VOSTAWORLD.COM

@ukelikethepros

INTERESTED IN **GUITAR CONTENT?**
ROCKLIKETHEPROS.COM

www.ingramcontent.com/pod-product-compliance
Lightning Source LLC
Chambersburg PA
CBHW081356040426
42451CB00017B/3472